The Death Camp Proved Him Real

The Death Camp Proved Him Real

The Life of Father Maximilian Kolbe, Franciscan

BY
MARIA
WINOWSKA

PROW
8000 - 39th Avenue
Kenosha, WI 53141

Nihil Obstat: Edward A. Cerny, S.S., D.D.
         Censor librorum

Imprimatur: Most Reverend Francis P. Keough, D.D.
         Archbishop of Baltimore

January 31, 1952

The nihil obstat and imprimatur are official declarations
that a book or pamphlet is free of doctrinal and moral
error. No implication is contained therein that those who
have granted the nihil obstat and imprimatur agree with
the opinions expressed.

This biography of Fr. Maximilian Kolbe, translated by Therese
Plumereau from the French, was first published by The New-
man Press in 1952 under the title **Our Lady's Fool.** This new
American edition has been revised, and enlarged with the addition of a new "Epilogue" written for it by the author. The latter
was translated by Jacqueline Bowers and Rev. Bernard M.
Geiger, O.F.M.Conv.

DECLARATION

Conforming to the decree of Pope Urban VIII, the author declares that all she has written in this biography is based only on the certitude of human testimony.

Io voglio mandarvi tutti in paradiso.
St. Francis of Assisi

Preface

For centuries, Christian dogmas have been subjected to attack, while unanimous homage of a sort has been conceded to Christian morality. However, the ideologies of our day cast blame upon the gospel ideal itself.

Speeches are of little value to imbue our contemporaries with this ideal. They can be convinced only by living examples of the force of divine love, by witnesses to Christian values who hail from their own towns, share their labors, their dangers, their sufferings, their enthusiasms also—but witnesses who radiate an abundant life which astonishes these men and appears to be a manifestation of God. Our contemporaries wait for saints.

Here is one who comes from Poland. He had an unlimited ambition: to save *all* souls. To realize his ambition he vowed himself to the *Immaculata* with an allegiance which was likewise unlimited.

Men today cannot disavow this son of Saint Francis of Assisi under the pretext that he sanctified himself in a medieval framework; for, with the exception of its sins, he loved all of the modern world and he conscripted for God the printing press, the radio, the airplane. And he knew all its miseries too: tuberculosis, bombings, enemy occupation, prison camp—the concentration camp of Oswiecim (Auschwitz).

A sainted prisoner! The story of his death with which this book ends is at once one of the most dreadful and the most sublime that a book from a human pen could yield. In that last circle of the hell-like concentration camp, where men strove to dehumanize other men before killing them, he freely offered his life for another, wresting from the executioners this word of amazement: "The like of this we have never seen!"

BRUNO OF SOLAGES

Rector of the Catholic
Faculties of Toulouse

Contents

Prologue:

Can Christian Love Survive a Death Camp?

I start with a confession. Where did I get the idea to write this book? Why have I written it?

Father Maximilian Kolbe has haunted me ever since a day toward the end of the war when I was lodged at the Abbey of Montserrat in Spain. Like so many others in flight from the secret police, I had been forced to cross the Pyrenees. I found a brief notice of his death in my mail forwarded from Jerusalem. I knew from experience what the concentration camp is—the forced labor, the hunger. I also knew how certain unaccepted sufferings degrade. Death does not improvise itself. Death is the last note of a life's whole theme. So I asked myself the question: "What was the profound life of this religious man that he chose to die in that way?"

I had got little more than a glimpse of him. Frail, his head slightly bent, his looks were not impressive. People had introduced him to me as a powerful man of action, enthusiastic, enterprising. I was struck by the penetrating and limpid expression of his eyes. I knew vaguely of *Niepokalanow*, "the City of the Immaculata," which he had built in the wilderness. I confess it: he mystified me; but my academic work could scarcely place me in contact with his publications.

War came. Hunted by the Germans, I was obliged to leave Poland secretly. Here again Father Maximilian was following me into Spain by way of Jerusalem. I began by writing an article in Spanish, published in *Cristiandad* at Barcelona. In France I wrote a brief biographical essay in *La Vie Spirituelle*. Then I thought that Father Maximilian and I would part company. But no! The saint would not relax his grip easily. He kept haunting me—I mean as a subject for a book.

Still I hesitated. It is not easy to make a saint live again, and in a language which is not yours! If only I could write in Polish, using words altogether familiar and easy to manage . . . But the French language in strange hands often balks as does a beautiful pony on the open plain, with moist eyes and snorting nostrils, obeying only his master. I definitely preferred to evade the attempt.

Here is the incident which made me succumb after so many hesitations. Without a conversation with Pierre, who had been imprisoned in the same camp as I—his name is different, but that does not matter—this book would not have been written. Pierre and I met on a Paris boulevard one day in the spring. There was a light rain, and trees were in bloom. Our discussion became a trifle heated, with the result that I had to give up, accept the challenge, and take to writing. Pierre had spent four years in the concentration camp of Dachau. He had come back bitter, aged, unrecognizable; his body sick, his soul still more sick. At each one of our meetings, it was the same story: "I no longer have any faith in man. What a filthy beast he is! What a selfish brute!"

His memories obsessed him. He sipped the bitterness of their horror, scrutinizing one by one the long line of miseries. He would finish by hissing through his teeth the horrible words of Sartre: "Human fellowship is hell!"

To a very direct question, he gave this answer: "Yes, I believe that God exists, in an inaccessible heaven of heavens, while we poor human beings are crawling in mud. Grace?

Why, yes, that exists perhaps, but of what importance is it if it does not succeed in changing man? There are certain miseries where grace has no access, where even God conceals His face. If you only knew!"

"Tell me, Pierre," I said to him, "what do you make of the saints?"

He began to laugh, a laugh that hurt. "Why, yes, I believe in saints. I believe that there are saints. But they are products of greenhouses. They need a special climate, a favorable one with sanctifying conditions. Saints do not grow in inhuman soil. I defy you to show me a saint in a concentration camp. One saint. One who truly prefers his neighbor to himself. I defy you!"

For a moment I kept silent. Then, "Pierre, suppose I accept the challenge? If I show you a saint in a real concentration camp; someone who offered to die in place of a fellow prisoner . . . "

He looked at me with his pitiful beaten-dog eyes. We were standing in a doorway, while the rain fell hard and the brisk steps of infrequent passers-by alternated with the gusts of rain.

"Then, and only then, will I admit that you are right."

We changed the subject, but the blow had reached its mark. From this broken conversation the scheme of this book originated. It is not intended especially for religious persons, neither for the convents nor for the ladies of charitable societies. I destine and dedicate it to my brother the condemned one, to all those who have lost faith in man and, through that loss, no longer believe in God!

Every man is an image of the living God, but only the saint appraises it, as a jeweler appraises a pearl. We have the terrible power to spit into the adorable Face, slap It, twist It into a caricature. The saint carries It as in a living monstrance. And a time can come when the invading Presence flashes like a flame on the bruised body, making sacred wounds blossom. Not every saint bears the stigmata; but there is no saint who does not die on the Cross. Love must be stronger than death. And sanctity is simply an adventure of love, the most thrilling adventure, *and within reach of all*. This is what Father Maximilian Kolbe, whose life I here relate, was incessantly preaching.

1

Where It All Began:
The Two Crowns

The parents of Raymond Kolbe were poor people, plain weavers who worked hard in order to live. In Poland at that time, a working day was ten hours long. The salaries were meager and left to the will of the middlemen, who resold with enormous profits the beautiful fabrics manufactured with great care and love in innumerable small workshops. The large industry of Lodz was just coming into existence. The workingman would labor in his home fully under the control of these exploiters. By working together continually for ten hours a day, husband and wife would earn just enough to raise a family.

Jules Kolbe was tall, blond, very gentle, a little taciturn; he did not drink or smoke, and attended church frequently. Through these qualities, he won the heart and hand of his wife Maria, whose maiden name was Dabrowska. From her we get a more accurate picture. She left us several letters written in a high-flown style and with an unskilled hand, but full of touching details.

Maria as a child seemed to have a religious vocation. But at that time—we are in 1875—the Russian occupation had suppressed the convents; the nuns were scattered and did not wear any distinctive garb. Maria did not know any of them but prayed naïvely that she might die before being obliged to marry. However, it does not appear that when she did marry she felt that she had made a great sacrifice. She chose her future willingly, delighted to see her husband so virtuous—and so docile, because (may the Lord forgive me!) it seems to me that it was she who vigorously conducted all the business of the poor household. Energetic, pious, a little gossipy, a hard worker, very quick at getting out of a fix, she ruled her little world masterfully and could not tolerate disobedience. I find her a little harsh, but grace will smooth out such flaws.

Evidently, with boys—and there were only boys—a firm hand was necessary. Two had died very young; there were three others: Francis, Raymond, the subject of this book (born January 8, 1894, and Joseph, the youngest. Perhaps she was a little too firm. When punishments for mischief were coming to him, Raymond, a very honest lad, would stretch over the bench and hold out the whip to his mother. He accepted peacefully what he deserved and then repeated his mischievous acts again and again. Fortunately, he was a child like others and, according to numerous witnesses, a very winning little boy.

He loved nature and entertained himself by planting little trees. One day, after his ordination, he was to come back to Pabianice to see "his trees." They are still standing. Here is the worst misdeed recorded of him. One day, with his own money he bought an egg and put it under a hen to be hatched. He wanted so much to have a little chick! Unfortunately his mother did not agree with him, and the little Raymond received a sound beating. Had he forgotten to ask permission? It is most likely that the person who hands this incident down to us forgot to quote the aggravating circumstances, for Raymond was not yet a saint. He was not even a child of an easy temper, if we can believe certain scattered remarks. Lively, very independent, enterprising and stubborn, with a brisk and impulsive nature, he tried the patience of his mother, who one day exclaimed in exasperation, 'My poor child, what will become of you?"

Her expression must have been more eloquent than the words she spoke with joined hands and eyes uplifted to heaven, for this reprimand brought on the little one a real crisis of soul. His mother admitted that from that time he changed completely and became very good and very obedient. Surprised at this sudden transformation, she began to watch the lad and noticed that he disappeared more and more often behind the cupboard, where there was a little altar of Our Lady of Czestochowa with an oil-lamp which was lighted every Wednesday, Saturday and Sunday. Crouched in the corner, the child prayed a long time and would come out with his eyes reddened by tears. Very much puzzled, his mother one day subjected him to close questioning.

"Now then, Raymond, what is the matter with you? Why do you cry like a girl?" She thought he was sick.

Raymond hung his head and did not want to answer.

Fortunately, she insisted and broke through to that fierce, shy little soul! She took the most effective way.

"Look here, my little one, you must tell everything to Mother; do not be disobedient!"

"Oh, no," Raymond thought, "for nothing in the world would I give up obedience, now that I have seen her."

Crying and trembling, he spoke. "Mother, when you said to me, 'Raymond, what will become of you?' I felt very sad and went to the Blessed Virgin and asked her what would become of me. After that, in church I asked her again. Then the Blessed Virgin appeared to me, holding two crowns; one white and the other red. She looked lovingly at me and asked me which one I would choose. The white one meant that I would always be pure, and the red one that I would die a martyr. Then I answered the Blessed Virgin, 'I choose both of them.' She smiled and disappeared.

"Since then," he added after a moment of silence, "when we go to church, it seems to me that I no longer go with Father and you, but with the Blessed Virgin and Saint Joseph.

Like a good psychologist, his mother explains: "His radical transformation proves that the child was telling the truth. From that day he was not the same. His face aglow, he would often talk to me of martyrdom, his great dream."

Was this a mystical experience such as one meets in the life of guileless children—the kind grown-ups fortunately fail to grasp? Was this high grace and prophetic vision? That is not for us to decide. But above all, let us not lose sight of one fact: this little boy was nothing of a dreamer. Rather, he was precise, concrete, deeply realistic, so passionately interested in modern technical discoveries that he excelled in the sciences.

The crisis of his soul once solved, he was never again to mention the mysterious meeting. For long years, until his death, Raymond guarded the secret jealously. All his life was to be set and illuminated by it, but he confided it to no one. It took an emphatic order from his mother to make him speak. After that, absolute silence. Only once, shortly before his death, did the secret flow to his lips, but an invincible reserve prevented his telling it. Even then, he reproached himself for having "talked too much." Despite his open-hearted nature, joyful and sincere, he never confided it to anyone. At the age of ten—for he was only ten at the time—his heart was captured forever. She was there. She was enough. His Confidant, his Queen, and his Lady.

2

How to Achieve
An Impossible Dream

Raymond meanwhile grew like the little trees he planted. All the testimonies we have been able to gather attest to the fact that he was charming. Since the great crisis of his soul, he had become perfectly well-behaved and made visible effort to get rid of his petty childhood defects. He was also very intelligent, but no one knew that yet.

Like so many poor people, his parents had not the means to pay for his education. They taught the children how to read and write from the little they knew themselves. Finally, by great effort they sent Francis, the oldest boy and the favorite, to the business school of Pabianice. As for Raymond, he had to stay home and help his family.

His mother was doing all she could to supplement the too meager wages of her husband. She started a little shop where she sold herrings, sauerkraut, garlic, candles, shoelaces, and all the odds and ends necessary in the poor surroundings. Young Raymond had a head for figures and was soon able to replace her. She also worked as a midwife. Often she would be called away while she was preparing meals. During her absence Raymond was in charge of the family cooking and managed very well. His mother tells us that he used to invent the most tasty dishes and often welcomed her with "a surprise." As an old woman, she still spoke of this with tears in her eyes.

Under these conditions, it seemed more and more evident that little Raymond's dreams would never be realized. He seemed made to measure goods and tend the counter.

It was significant that he never expressed his great desire; he simply obeyed. From that time, and probably since the apparition, we see him peacefully and often heroically submissive to the mysterious guidance of Providence. Throughout his life this was a striking fact, and it must be attributed to a special grace which coincided, perhaps, with his wonderful "meeting" with Our Lady. All favorites of the Blessed Virgin are heroes of obedience, reproducing her redemptive fiat in their lives even unto the supreme sacrifice. This is their mark of election. Evidently young Raymond did not know all that. The Blessed Virgin had not given him theological courses, but we can imagine her leaning over the little boy, telling him: "Do all they tell you and I will do the rest."

Providence arrived unexpectedly in the person of a pharmacist whose name was Kotowski. One day Madame Kolbe sent her little boy for the medicine of one of her nursing cases. Raymond, who had a very good memory, rattled off in one breath the Latin formula. The pharmacist looked at him a little disconcerted and asked, "How do you know what it is called?"

It would have been sufficient to answer that he was repeating word for word what his mother had said to him, but the child, proud of the impressive effect, continued: "Father Jakowski teaches us Latin."

He was not yet a saint, and there was a note of conceit in his voice.

The pharmacist, delighted by this childish determination, continued to question him.

"That's all very well as far as Latin is concerned, but do you go to school?"

Then artlessly the boy confessed. "It's my older brother who goes to the business school. He is going to be a priest, but I have to remain at home to help my parents. There isn't enough money to send us both to school."

The pharmacist reflected for a moment. He liked the youngster. Then he made his decision.

"My boy, it is a shame to leave you this way. Come to my house and I will teach you. At the end of the year you will pass examinations with your brother."

Thanks to Mr. Kotowski, who with a word decided the future of Raymond Kolbe! Was he among those numberless obscure patriots who spent all their leisure time and energy teaching the children of the poor? Under the Russian occupation education was not free of charge. We know nothing about him except this fact and this intervention, which one day will bring him a little glory.

Raymond's delight proved too well how he had suffered from being unable to go to school. "He came back home as though he had wings," wrote his mother, "and at once related to me the marvelous good fortune that had befallen him."

Mr. Kotowski had seen aright. The youngster worked so hard that he caught up with his brother's studies and succeeded in his examinations. Then his parents decided to make even greater effort and sent him also to school.

According to the testimony of a schoolmate, Raymond was the most talented in his class, excelling chiefly in mathematics and solving all problems as if he were playing a game. "He was talented in everything."

Mrs. Kolbe continued to govern her boys with an iron hand. There was to be no playing truant! Chatting with girls was forbidden. We learn that the oldest son, Francis, was too much inclined to this frivolity. After the boys had studied their lessons, they had to help in the house so that not a moment would be lost.

Four years later, the Franciscan Fathers came to Pabianice to preach a mission and at the same time to recruit vocations. Gathering all the courage they could, Francis and Raymond went to the priests and asked admission to the Minor Seminary of Lwow. We do not know the details, but one fact is clear: the parents were in perfect accord with the idea. Their father accompanied them to Cracow in the Austrian zone. To reach it, they had to cross the frontier secretly, a maneuver familiar to the Poles since the partitioning of their fatherland. From Cracow, they took the train to Lwow. They were travelling alone for the first time in their lives and their hearts were beating hard! It was the beginning of the term of 1907. Raymond was thirteen years of age.

3

Can a Warrior Wear a Friar's Habit?

At that time Lwow was the capital of Galicia, which comprised, under an assumed name, the provinces of Poland annexed by Austria. While applying a clever system of "progressive assimilation," the emperors, many of whom were Catholics, respected the religious convictions of their subjects. The convents, stifled for a long time, started to take on a new vigor. Almost all the novitiates were in that zone, and they trained missionaries who would one day secretly cross the frontier to labor in the Russian or the German zone. The friary of the Franciscans called Conventuals (who date back in direct line to their holy founder, Francis of Assisi) was recovering little by little from a long decline. The recruiting was good and the missionaries were continually coming back from the "Kingdom," as they called the Russian zone, with new candidates.

Raymond continued his studies. He took a deep interest in mathematics and the sciences. He was the pride of his comrades and the terror of his professors, who were tried by his ingenuity in posing difficulties, not through malice but simple curiosity. Very soon he clearly displayed real genius as an inventor. During walks he enjoyed making clever calculations, planned interplanetary flights, and related to his amazed schoolmates how he would one day build an apparatus to go to the moon.

He loved making strategic plans. One day in a public garden he sketched a system of fortifications which would make Lwow impregnable. He had invented a game in which no one could follow him. With bits of wood he had made series of pawns—his strategic units—and for hours he would place them on a complicated chessboard, opposing two invisible armies. Once during an extremely delicate maneuver a companion in passing rudely upset the battlefield. Raymond turned red with anger, tears in his eyes; but he knew how to control himself and said nothing. Here was fine strength of character for a fifteen-year-old boy! Childish, very childish in his games, he was amazing in his exceptional maturity. He will not cease to amaze us.

Raymond undoubtedly had soldier's blood in his veins, as do the Polish people generally, and displayed an obvious inclination for the military life. "If he had not joined the Friars," declared one of his schoolmates, "he would surely have become a great strategist or a clever inventor."

And it is here that the second crisis of soul took place.

He was just sixteen years of age, and it was time to decide whether he would enter the novitiate. But Raymond hesitated. He honestly believed that he could bring a soldier's life into perfect harmony with that of the knight entirely consecrated to the Queen of his heart!

It is to be understood that this crisis of soul had nothing to do with a crisis of the senses. In his child's heart he was already dreaming of grand conquests. But are not all conquerors soldiers? As a friar would he be capable of such prowess? He decided to go to Father Provincial and tell him that he would not stay, that he did not feel he had the call to the religious life.

Once more Providence intervened. At the very moment when he was going to the Father Provincial, he was called to the visiting parlor. It was his mother glowing with excitement over the news she had for him. Following the example of the two older sons, the third one, Joseph, had decided to become a religious also. Furthermore, she and Mr. Kolbe had decided to enter the service of religion and follow their life-long attraction. The father had already gone to Cracow, to the Franciscan Friars. She was going to Lwow to join the Benedictine Sisters. Now the *whole* family would belong to God!

It was a thunderclap for Raymond.

How could he confess his intentions at such a moment? Was what he wanted really the will of God? Was he not merely in the mood to listen to a temptation? Suddenly his eyes were opened; he felt himself at the edge of a precipice. As soon as his mother had gone, he ran "fleet as an arrow" to the Father Provincial and breathlessly asked him for the Franciscan religious habit. All his life he would remember this memorable incident which decided his vocation. Nine years later, he was to speak of it again to his mother, in a letter from Rome.

We shall see that grace, like an expert gardener, pruned these desires and these talents only to give them a more beautiful blossoming. More than once in his wonderful life Raymond was to have the occasion to perform the roles of soldier, knight and commander. And he would die a martyr, a martyr of war. At the moment the future was befogged. Only one thing was asked of him—to sacrifice all. He did it with all his heart, but with a bleeding heart.

His entrance into the novitiate was followed by a very painful ordeal. For a few months he suffered an attack of scruples of conscience, a dreadful distress of soul which rooted him even more firmly in obedience, the only remedy for this malady. His companion and roommate in the novitiate, Friar Bronislaw, was charged by the Master of Novices to help him. A hundred times a day the poor novice would come to submit the state of his soul and blindly obey. This heroic obedience saved him. The storm passed; serenity came back to his soul. But he acquired experience which gave him an angelic patience with scrupulous penitents in later years.

His novitiate served to replace little by little "the old man" by "the new man." *Obiit Raymundus, natus est Maximilianus:* Raymond has died; Maximilian is born. We do not know to what Raymond owed his religious name. He probably did not choose it himself, but it is as Maximilian that he will be known in history.

The apprenticeship of holiness is made much more through example than through books. Friar Maximilian had the good fortune to meet a young religious who was known for his heroic virtue and who died at an early age in the odor of sanctity, Father Venance Katarzyniec. They were together only a short time during the 1912 vacation, but the young novice watched him closely and later wrote of him pages trembling with emotion. After vacation Father Venance left for Cracow, but his brief stay left the novitiate of Lwow scented with holiness. Maximilian was impressed by two things: the strict observance of this very delicate friar, already in the grip of his fatal illness; and an extreme humility that equalled his remarkable talents. The eighteen-year-old novice would live by that lesson.

In 1911, he pronounced his temporary vows. In the autumn of 1912 his superiors, recognizing his exceptional abilities, decided to send him to Rome to attend the Gregorian University. He should have rejoiced, but he did not. With tears in his eyes, he asked the Father Provincial to remove his name from the list. The astonished Provincial complied. But after sleeping on it, Friar Maximilian asked himself with anguish whether he had not exercised his own will in preference to God's as manifested in the desires of his superiors. Is it not better to give way blindly to His will and simply obey? He went back to the Provincial, declared he was prepared to go, and again was put on the list.

I was very much puzzled while reading this episode and for a long time asked myself the reasons for his refusal and violent repugnance to a sojourn which should have fascinated him. Finally I found the answer in one of his letters to his mother.

Had they not crammed his mind with fantastic stories, making him believe that "in Rome women accosted the monks in the middle of the street and constantly harassed them"? Friar Maximilian at eighteen was a handsome young man. In certain kinds of temptation flight is the only remedy. He would prefer not to confront these terrible women, but since obedience commanded it . . . In the last letter to his mother before his departure for Rome, he heavily underlined his request:

"I ask you, Mother, to pray for me *in a very special way,* because I need it greatly; down there in Rome, there are dangers, very serious dangers. I understand that some women accost even the religious, and yet it will indeed be necessary to go out in order to attend the courses."

The letter is dated October 28, 1912. He arrived in Rome on November 10; and the idea of "dangerous women" must have haunted him very much, for in his first letter to his mother, dated November 21, he wrote, "Things are not so terrible as I thought when I wrote you. Would the Italian women really have nothing better to do than to accost us? Besides, we always go out in groups."

The idea is amusing and significant. This malicious slander concerning Italian women had been necessary to reveal the purity of this young friar. Rather than endanger

the white virtue so long consecrated to his "Lady," he preferred to give up the opportunity to study in Rome. But genuine obedience prefers nothing. It was at Rome that Providence waited for him.

4

The Message of Rome

SAINTS ARE NOT MADE IN A DAY
THE ROLE OF THE IMMACULATA

Rome was a decisive and formidable experience. At the crossroads of time and eternity, Rome sees from aloft, sees afar. Whoever approaches her honestly sees himself gradually reduced to his true proportions, like a tree trimmed by wise and patient pruning. Rome goes straight to the heart of human beings and things, scoffs at excess, aims only at the essential. Has it not received as inheritance the golden reed, the standard of truth, mentioned in the Apocalypse? To face Rome, you must consent to "be what you are," according to the famous words of Pindar brought to our attention by the unforgettable Charles Du Bos.

The chattering group of young Polish friars, recently disembarked, did not read openly the mute interrogation on these walls addressed to each one of them. They did not know how to penetrate the invitation to greatness proposed to them by the Palatine which stood solemnly attentive before their windows. They lived at the International College of the Order on the street of San Teodoro, which skirts the venerable hill. No briefing had preceded their arrival. They knew only one thing: the Pope is in Rome, at the heart of Christendom. Was this not the important thing? Rome, the patient educator, would do all the rest.

The letters of Friar Maximilian to his mother, the only firsthand documents which remain from this time, are—let us say it frankly—banal. The young friar looks, observes sharp-eyed, and describes what he has seen with the same sense of precise detail which always characterized him. By no means do we feel he is overwhelmed by the surrounding greatness. Like a young tree in spring, he provides himself with strength. Assimilation will come little by little. At eighteen, one does not possess the sense of history. Gradually, however, the style changes. Emotion is stifled by awkward wordings. Anyone who reads between lines distinctly perceives that there is a process of deepening going on. Grace does not rest, and for its expansion it found a singularly responsive nature in this young friar.

In passing let us note a few details. Holy Week at Saint Peter's and the solemn benediction with Veronica's Veil: "I asked my companion to lend me his glasses. I looked and it happened that Jesus' face appeared to me, truly, miraculously printed on the veil." The visit to the Colosseum. On this soil dyed red with martyrs' blood, did he recall the promise of the two crowns? The touching description of the solemn consecration of the Franciscan Order to the Sacred Heart. The blessing of the Holy Father *urbi et orbi*. About himself he wrote nothing, not the least personal confidence—and he was writing to his mother whom he loved tenderly! Did he want to put someone on the wrong scent? Did he not know how to express himself? Perhaps he shared the habit of all the children of our country, who only *describe* what they have seen and never speak about the things which touch them most intimately. I rather believe that he expressed himself very well, but that the singular modesty of his deeply secretive soul prevented his revealing himself to others. The testimonies of his companions at that time show us a very different

Friar Maximilian. They all agree on one point: he was a saint.

I will once more assume the role of the Devil's Advocate. Testimonies about a period long since past are illumined by the light of more recent deeds, so that alleged virtues tend to borrow that new light and give to insignificant details an importance they did not possess. The ascent toward sanctity is painstaking and is not made in one day. Let us not confuse the scheme of things. In 1913 Friar Maximilian was not yet a saint, although passionately taken with sanctity. Let us not try to set the date of the accomplishment; it is a secret of the Holy Spirit. Let us be satisfied with knowing one thing: namely, that grace has its methods and respects the laws of growth. I remember an eminent theologian who once told me, "At the seminary we had the custom of saying, 'He lies like a second nocturn!' " Why? Because earlier hagiography presents the saints to us as *having arrived* and never as being *on the way*.

Yet, Friar Maximilian was "on the way"—and with a very good start.

The only letter of that time which deserves our special attention is dated April 6, 1914. It is composed of two parts, the first of which seems to me particularly important because it reveals to us certain facts of his intimate life and, if I dare say, of his spirituality.

For Easter he sent his mother this greeting, "I will wish you, Mother, neither health nor prosperity. Why? Because I want to wish you better than that, something so good that God Himself would not wish you better: that in all things, the will of this very good Father be accomplished in you, Mother, that you may know in all things how to fulfill the will of God! This is the very best I wish for you. God Himself could not wish better than that."

It is a total program of spiritual life that he proposes

here, a program which he had already begun to force into reality with his iron will. This young Franciscan with a round and candid face, with piercing and kindly eyes, was too smitten with the exact sciences to play with words. He took words very simply, literally, beginning with those of the gospel. And you may be sure that when he spoke he realized full well what he was saying.

The following episode is more striking. We quote in full this passage from one of his letters, because the later testimonies, including one of his mother's, have slightly exaggerated the incident. The fact, as the young friar relates it, is infinitely more touching.

"I very nearly lost the thumb of my right hand which had become infected by an abscess. In spite of our doctor's care, the pus was continually running. Finally the doctor declared that the bone was decaying and that the thumb would have to be amputated. However, I told him that I had a better remedy. In fact, the Father Rector had given me some blessed water from Lourdes and told me about his miraculous recovery. At the age of twelve he had a diseased foot; the bone was putrefying. He could not sleep and would scream with pain. Finally, they decided to amputate. That same evening the doctors were to hold a consultation. Seeing what was going on, his mother decided on another remedy. She took off all the plasters, washed the diseased foot with soap, and applied a compress of Lourdes water. For the first time, the Father Rector was able to sleep. After a quarter of an hour, he awoke—cured. The miracle was evident. The doctor, who was an unbeliever, tried to explain it away. However, when after a few days a piece of rotted bone came loose and emerged from the sole of the foot, the doctor had to admit that this bone was putrefying and that the cure had been miraculous. He was converted and had a church built at his expense.

"Now, when our doctor learned that I had some water from Lourdes he readily agreed that I use it. What happened? The next day at the hospital, the surgeon told me that an operation was not strictly necessary. After several dressings, I was cured. Glory to God and thanks to the Immaculata!"

The cure was miraculous. All the witnesses agree on this point. But was it a mere coincidence that his program of spiritual life, already outlined in a masterly manner, coincided with the announcement of his cure? Visitors at Lourdes know very well the methods of the Blessed Virgin. The physical cures are for publicity, if one may say so. But often these are infinitely surpassed by accompanying spiritual graces which escape the grasp of our limited knowledge. The letter to his mother is the first of Friar Maximilian's writings in which he uses the concise term *the Immaculata*. The name consecrated by centuries of use in Poland is *Matka Boska* (Mother of God). To introduce into current language the title glorifying her signal privilege, *Niepokalana* (the Immaculata), required no less than a minor linguistic revolution; and Maximilian was destined to be its ardent promoter. He had found the Immaculata in Rome!

The year 1914 was for him a year of graces. On November 1, All Saints' Day, he took his solemn vows, that splendid act of a devoted soul, that call for a courageous climb to sanctity. The young friar with a precise mind, much taken up with logic and pursuing all things to their ultimate conclusions, felt himself placed by profession squarely on the road to perfection. Powerful graces helped him. It was at that time that his slow transformation began. Like a chrysalis, little by little he grew the butterfly's wings. Nothing now would stop his soaring.

In the meantime war had broken out, proving for the young religious a powerful lever and the beginning of a great pity for souls. For it is of a truth that for those who love God all things work together unto good—even war. The First World War matured him; the Second glorified him! The wonderful story of his life was bound between two wars.

5

A New Army for the
Warrior Queen

All his Polish comrades, being Austrian subjects, were obliged to leave Italy. Possessing a Russian passport, Friar Maximilian was interned for a few weeks in San Marino and then permitted to enter Rome. At San Teodoro they read the daily communiqués. The Rector of the Seminary, Father Stephen Ignudi, did not fail to relate after each of his visits to the Vatican the great sorrow of the Pope, of whom he was the confidant and friend. The Christian family of nations was torn to pieces by fratricidal war. Could there be greater anguish for a Father's heart? At the International College of San Teodoro, young and old shared in this inexpressible mourning.

Friar Maximilian had no taste for empty ideas. He was not satisfied with words. The Church was suffering. The Pope was suffering. The powers of evil were unchained and the infernal offensive battered in positions which had seemed invincible. Christian charity stopped short and yielded before the barbed lines. Even the priests no longer dared to talk of love for the enemy. Was it the time to remain in the corner, idle and passive? Was it not necessary, rather, to prepare and attempt a counterattack, to weigh well the methods, and to choose effective weapons and impregnable positions? There, Friar Maximilian, was your opportunity to devise a clever strategy! To devise a plan and engage in battle! Engage in battle—and conquer! For he who would stop halfway is lost; the program minutely mapped out must be pursued *to the end*.

Friar Maximilian meditated upon this and prayed. As a child he had amused himself by setting up a strategic defense of Lwow, "the city of eaglets." The task he now proposed to himself was in a very different way overwhelming. All Christendom was in danger. Souls were being led astray. It was necessary to save *all* these souls! He was a soldier at heart, and the Lady of his heart was a Warrior Virgin. In Poland, devotion to the Virgin Mary is born at the bugles' blast! *Cunctas haereses sola interemisti.** The conclusion, drawn according to good traditional logic, is this: With her as ally, *the victory is certain*.

I make not the slightest pretention of reproducing the progress of ardent thought within this twenty-year-old religious. I very simply point out the principal stages. Already, Friar Maximilian was what he would always be, a man with a logic like steel. Rarely could we find a spirit less dreamy than this. If he saw a thing to do, if he was sure that it was the will of God, nothing in the world could prevent his undertaking it. On the buttress of such a fidelity, grace could build. The Warrior Queen had wisely chosen her knight.

The Mariological environment of the International College, the great Franciscan tradition, and the solid theological studies guided and clarified what had been, from the start, the secret attraction of his soul. In these surroundings he merely followed his fundamental principles to their logical conclusions.

Mary is the Immaculate Conception. The promulgation

*"You alone have crushed all heresies."

of this dogma has clothed with glory the Franciscan Order, which had propounded it for centuries. Must we not now draw from this dogma all its practical implications, living for it as well as having contributed to its promulgation? And does not the promulgation of this unique privilege call for the consequent recognition of Mary as the Mediatrix of all graces?

Mary's immaculate conception caused an implacable enmity to arise between her and man's ancient adversary, the Devil, and thus constituted her THE WOMAN promised by the Father in the Garden of Eden.* By it Mary was able to join intimately in her Son's mortal struggle against Satan, sin and death, and thus share completely both in His victory, and in the royal power won by right of conquest. As Warrior Queen, and Mother of the King, she dispenses the treasures of the Kingdom by right.

From Christ, then, and through her, all grace comes to us. With capacity only for God, she lives only through Him, works only for Him, wants only Him. Delegate of the Infinite Mercy, she is the crucible in which all our dross is consumed by the flame of that sacrificial love, which, to make a worthy offering, accepts only the purest gold. As Mother of Christ, she will not know how to bestow her sublime grace upon us without fashioning yet other Christs. Mother of the Head, therefore Mother of the Mystical Body, and Mother of the entire Christ, she receives only to give and takes only to transform. There is only one obstacle insuperably destructive of her redemptory action—our voluntary refusal of it. But, on the contrary, an unqualified *fiat,* as unconditional as hers, makes us participate in her all-powerful suppliance. Mother of all graces, what could she refuse to the one who would be all to her: her son, her knight, her servant? All that

---

*Genesis 3, 15.

matters is to surrender to her sanctifying action, to be a ready instrument in her radiant hands. She, the Immaculata, is the direct way to Christ, the weapon of conquest with which to establish the reign of Christ, the perfect way of giving Christ.

All these thoughts Friar Maximilian never tired of rehearsing, of setting off in even higher relief, of delving into more and more deeply. At the moment, he could not state them precisely; he discovered them little by little, on his knees. Later on, he often said to his sons that we learn more about the Blessed Virgin in praying than we do in reading; we learn more bowed down before her than bent over learned books.

The years spent in Rome were a sowing time and gave him priceless experience. As formerly with Joan of Arc, he needed a council in which the important figures were, not only the "Commander in Chief," but an entire staff of saints, "especially those who were particularly devoted to Mary." The day of his first Mass, he was even to make a pact with Thérèse of Lisieux, as yet not canonized, telling her, "I will pray that you may be elevated to the glory of the altars, but provided that you take charge of all my future conquests." There were no conquests yet, but does not a good general make sure of his effective forces before signaling for the attack?

The confreres of Friar Maximilian would often come upon him engulfed in prayer in the chapel of the College. "When entering, one would think there was no one there, but after some time would hear a slight noise. It was he—hidden behind the high altar . . . I was impressed by his contemplative quiet during the morning meditation," the same witness adds. "His whole attitude betrayed a powerful inner activity."

I convey this awkward wording purposely; it shows wonderfully well the impression made on his companions.

Everyone took him for a contemplative, and that he was. But this aptitude for prayer was coupled with the most remarkable qualities of a man of action. This contemplation of his overflowed into works of the highest technical competence. Qualities so apparently contradictory have rarely concurred in a more harmonious balance. I will even say that harmony was his striking feature. In order to find another example, we would have to go back to the Poverello or Saint Bernard. But let us not anticipate. While on his knees behind the altar, the young student was on the way to acquiring grades much more difficult than those of the Gregorian University, where he passed his examinations brilliantly. In the school of the Holy Spirit promotion is equivalent to living the Beatitudes.

Friar Maximilian learned very quickly, and at his own expense, the ABC's of the science of the saints as summarized by Raymond Lully in the phrase, "To love is to suffer." Scarcely had he conceived his grandiose plan to rescue the world, when the test fell upon him with its full weight. First came blood spittings, then violent hemorrhages. He had never been in very good health, and here was an illness which at his age does not spare. It was possible that he was dangerously stricken, perhaps lost. He did not worry over his health; nor did his friends. There were certain exemptions, a few more walks—that was all! Among the memoirs and testimonies I did not find the slightest reference to regular medical treatment. For consumptive people, Rome is fatal; but he stayed in Rome, except during summer vacations. His sickness occurred in the summer of 1917. It is striking that his colleagues, even those who had the greatest regard for him, scarcely speak about it. Someone who had observed him closely even tried to convince me that he had not been ill at Rome!

We should refrain from passing judgment, above all on

his superiors. They surely would have cared for him attentively had they known the gravity of his illness. The only guilty one, I think, is Friar Maximilian himself. He did not talk about his ailment. He did not bother with it and was even pleased with the idea of going to heaven, perhaps soon. In the meantime he was preparing a plan of conquest capable of absorbing a whole lifetime. Sublime inconsistency! In order to know really what was taking place in his heart, it would have been necessary to intercept his silent prayer behind the high altar.

Let us listen to what he himself relates in an unpublished and revealing testimony written in 1935 by order of the Guardian, Father Florian Koziura. This document takes on even greater value since it is the *only one* in which he speaks directly of himself.

"How did the Militia of the Immaculata originate? Much time has glided by since then, almost eighteen years. I have, therefore, forgotten a great many details. . . . "

Now then, Friar Maximilan, let me tease you a little. You have a good, an excellent, memory; but perhaps you simply do not want to say *too* much?

"Nevertheless, since Father Guardian orders me to describe the beginnings of the Militia of the Immaculata, I will write what I still remember.

"Well, I recall that I would often chat with my confreres on the lack of enthusiasm of some within the Order and of the future of the Order. It is then that these words were impressed on my mind, 'Refuse to compromise, or we will destroy the Order!' " We remark that he does not tell us from whom these words came. Certain Fathers ascribe them to Father Ignudi, Rector of the College, an eminent religious, great ascetic and fervent supporter of the primitive observance.

"I am greatly affected by those young men who come to us with the highest ideals and sometimes dilute, while in the friary, their ideal of sanctity. So I thought: 'What can I do?'

"Let us look even farther back. I remember how, as a very young boy, I had bought a statuette of the Blessed Virgin for a few pennies. At the boarding school of Lwow during holy Mass, I prostrated myself face to the floor and promised the Blessed Virgin, who sat enthroned as Queen above the altar, *that I would go to battle for her.* I did not know yet how I was going to do it, but I envisioned a struggle with material arms.

"Then, when the time of novitiate arrived—or was it profession?—I confided this difficulty to the Prefect, Father Denis Sowiak, who commuted my promise to the obligation of reciting every day a *Sub tuum praesidium.** I recite it until this day, although I know now *what kind of battle the Immaculata had designs upon.*"

Friar Maximilian, do you not realize that in spite of yourself you have indeed said too much? Then it is the Immaculata who asked you to fight for her; then it is on her express order that you have appointed yourself her knight? What took place between you two at that memorable hour which determined your life? What sublime naïveté that you should then not know "what kind of battle the Immaculata had designs upon"! Neither did the Poverello know the full import of the order which summoned him to repair "My house falling into ruins." Francis of Assisi began simply to gather stones in order to restore Saint Damian's. You also have taken the order of the all-beautiful Virgin literally: "Since she asks me to fight, I will become a soldier." In listening to your soul, she must have smiled. Other struggles infinitely harder were awaiting you!

*A prayer to Mary beginning with the words, "We fly to your protection . . . "

In continuing his text Father Maximilian artlessly reveals even more of the inner secrets of his heart. "Although I had a strong inclination to pride, the attraction of the Immaculata was even more compelling. Above the prie-dieu in my cell I always had the picture of some saint to whom the Blessed Virgin had appeared. [How he betrays himself!] I often invoked these saints. Seeing one of these pictures, a certain friar remarked that I surely must have had a great devotion to that saint. . . . "

A delightful evasion. Friar Maximilian's pen has all the shyness of love. He would not have kept in mind this insignificant detail if he had not attached to it a certain importance. Was it not necessary to screen away from curious eyes that which in its recalling was bringing happiness to his heart? *Da mihi amantem et sentit quod dico!**

He continues. "The Freemasons began to spark their demonstrations with more and more effrontery, even raising their banners under the windows of the Vatican, banners which depicted on a black background Lucifer trampling underfoot the Archangel Michael. When they started to distribute vicious tracts against the Holy Father, the idea to establish a company to fight the Freemasons and other agents of Lucifer was born."

Friar Maximilian was not speaking of things which he had merely read in books; he witnessed them. To commemorate the second centenary of Freemasonry in 1917, Rome was chosen for the theater of their sacrilegious parodies. In Saint Peter's Plaza and in front of the windows of the august prisoner, bands of fanatics were brandishing the devilish banner bear the inscription: "Satan must reign in the Vatican; the Pope will be his slave."

Every evening the Father Rector related to the young

---

*"Show me the lover, and he will understand my words" (St. Augustine. Homily on St. John).

friars incidents which would have appeared stupid and grotesque if they had not been dictated by diabolical hatred. If God is Love, we know the name of the rebellious Angel! Placed in the heart of Christendom, the young religious of the Palatine were learning the mystery of evil no longer from books but by object lessons. The mind of Friar Maximilian retained the impression for life. It matters little that at that moment the enemy made himself chieftain of Freemasonry, to patronize twenty years later other wretched heresies. His name is Legion and he likes a change of label and of face, but his indelible sign is always the same—hatred of the just, hatred of the Church, hatred of the "Sweet Christ of the earth." It is against "the enemy," whatever his chameleon aspect, that our twenty-year-old friar declared war.

Incidentally, one cannot overlook the impersonal form of the modest statement: "the idea was born." Born to whom, Friar Maximilian? Since you are writing under orders of holy obedience, ought you not to tell us all?

"To completely reassure myself that this idea came from the Immaculata, I asked the opinion of my director, Father Alexander Basile, a Jesuit, who was the regular confessor of the students of the College. Having been reassured in the name of holy obedience, I decided immediately to start working."

Every word of this very simple text has its meaning. Necessarily so, for it is this grain of mustard which will become one day the great tree of a magnificent work.

In all she does the Blessed Virgin has a style which is utterly appropriate to her. She, who through obedience decided the work of Redemption, requires from all her chosen ones an absolute agreement, an unreserved docility, a heroic obedience. No need, Friar Maximilian, to confess to us that the Immaculata inspires you and guides you. In order to convince us this little text suffices: you do not want to undertake *anything* except in the name of holy obedience. I single out this trait purposely, because it is the distinctive mark of Friar Maximilian's spirituality. When the Church canonizes him some day—as we confidently expect—he may well be named "the Saint of holy obedience." There again the Warrior Queen delivers to him a weapon of unfailing power: only the absolute fiat, unconditional and whole, may subdue the one whose sin is summed up in these two words, *Non serviam!*[1] The knights of the Immaculata are by definition the heroes and, if needs be, the martyrs of obedience. On this score Maximilian the priest will place most implacable demands. One who does not know how to obey does not deserve to enter into the service of her of whom the greatest title of glory is to have been, to be always, "the servant of the Lord."

Thus he was an armed knight bearing, as it were, the title "Holy Obedience." What will be his first exploit, his first victory? Indeed, divine strategy differs singularly from human, and since God has established His reign from the height of the Cross—*Regnat a cruce Deus*[2]—how could His disciples dare hope for a treatment different from that inflicted upon the Master?

This young Polish friar's second mark of election was suffering. "Meanwhile we left to vacation in our 'country' house, 'La Vigna,' half an hour from the College.[3] One day, while we were playing football, I felt blood coming up to my lips. I stretched out on the grass. It was Father Biasi who took care of me. For a long time I spit blood. I was happy in the thought that perhaps it was the end! Afterwards, I went to see the doctor. He sent me back in a coach and

1. "I will not serve."
2. "God reigns from the cross."
3. The "Vigna" was not actually in the country but on a hill in the city overlooking the ruins of the ancient Baths of Caracalla; it was and still is, an area blessed with many open spaces.—Ed.

ordered me to go to bed immediately. Remedies did not succeed in stopping the continual hemorrhages. During these days, Father Jerome Biasi came to see me often."

At Rome I talked with Father Cicchito, who was Father Maximilian's prefect from 1912 to 1914. He told me that when the young friar had arrived from Poland, he had ruddy cheekbones and perpetually cold hands. In the wintertime his hands burst with painful chilblains which made him suffer very much, seeming to denote circulatory troubles or a cardiac defect. Father Cicchito took him to specialists, who gave divergent diagnoses; but there was no suspicion of tuberculosis prior to the outbreak of the war. I inquired about the food in wartime and was told that the friars did not suffer from too great privations. Moreover, there was no history of the disease in the Kolbe family. The inference, then, is that he contracted tuberculosis in Rome, and after 1914.

It is strange that in the evidence provided by those who had known him at the College *no one mentions* this very grave illness, which was on the point of taking him away. If we had not this document written and signed with his own hand, we would even be tempted to doubt that he was ill at all. All his associates agree that he *never* complained. One of his schoolfellows, Father Albert Arzilli, tells us of violent headaches from which Friar Maximilian frequently suffered; but, he adds, "Besides Father Rector and a few friars, no one even suspected. I knew he was having his most painful moments by the spasms which contracted his face."

His comrade and friend, Father Pal, does not even mention in his testimony the sickness which felled him. Nor does Father Pignalberi, one of the seven founders—and they were intimates. The dutiful Father Biasi, who was the confidant of his painful hours, carried with him to his grave Friar Maximilian's soul revelations, his delight in the thought that the day was perhaps near when he was going "to see *her*."

This phrase alluded perhaps to the French hymn to Our Lady with which he was so much taken, the one with the sweet refrain, "Some day I shall see her."

To prevent his immediate circle of friends from suspecting the extent of his suffering, he must have had a very simple and profound heroism. It takes that to renounce so thoroughly the sheer and basic instinct of self-preservation. In so doing, was he simply obeying the Immaculata? Was he not on the way to laying the foundations of a work which, to be divine, must be countersigned by the Cross? We are here in the "science of saints," which differs so much from our limited human prudence!

"After two weeks," Friar Maximilian calmly continues, "the doctor allowed me to go out for the first time. Accompanied by another cleric, Friar Assanna, I went with some difficulty to our place in the country. Seeing me, the friars started to cry with joy and brought me fresh figs, some wine and bread. I did not feel ill; the pains and hemorrhages had stopped. On that day, to Friar Jerome Biasi and Father Joseph Pal, who was ordained before me but attended the same course in theology, I first confided my plan to start a society. However, I set the condition that they would first ask the permission of their spiritual directors, so that we might be sure of the will of God."

One need know only a little psychology to see to what point the young and sickly friar was captivated by his idea that I dare to call "fixed." Are not all the saints divinely obsessed? And does not sanctity depend, after all, upon a faithful "yes" which in every test ratifies the crucifying commands of the Master? A youth with the prudence of mere nature would have said to grace, "Wait a little until I am in good health." Friar Maximilian took advantage of this first lull to spread his grandiose plans before his brothers.

I use purposely the daring adjective "grandiose." The

evidence and testimonies have laid too little emphasis upon the holy ambition of Father Maximilian. He viewed things on a grand scale. He wanted—ALL. He made plans of far-flung conquest. One day he remarked to a friend, "The Jesuits say: *Ad majorem Dei gloriam,** but I say: *Ad maximam Dei gloriam.*"*** It was not enough for him to say "more"; he had to use the superlative in all things—"because," he explained, "it alone is worthy of God."

He had not yet proved himself. His fiery words could be empty blustering. We know that not all of his schoolfellows were enthusiastic. Some would smile at his use of military terminology. For instance, he would say, "We will put the large pieces of artillery in motion; this or that will be our 420; the ejaculations to the Blessed Virgin will rout the enemy . . . " But not all of his comrades had his soldier's blood. Until his death, he liked to talk of his "engines of war" and carry in his pockets the famous "shells" intended to crush the enemy—an ample provision of miraculous medals.

Blessed are the pure of heart! They are the first to be conquered. Listen to the continuation. "When I felt a little better, they sent me to Viterbo for further rest with a comrade, Friar Anthony Glowinski. It is then that Father Glowinski entered the M.I. (Militia of Mary Immaculate). Soon after, we were joined by Friar Anthony Mansi, who has died since then, and Friar Henry Granata from the province of Naples.

"Besides these members, no one in the College suspected the existence of the M.I. Only the Rector, Father Stephen Ignudi, was acquainted with everything. The M.I. did nothing without his consent, because it is in obedience that the will of the Immaculata is made manifest." There it is, his *idée*

*"For the greater glory of God"—the Jesuit motto.
**"For the greatest glory of God."

fixe: obedience, obedience!—his fixed idea and invincible weapon.

Father Maximilian perhaps did not realize it, but he certainly gave his superiors difficult problems. Imagine yourself for an instant in their place. Here he is looking you right in the eyes with his frank and penetrating look and saying to you: "Command! In all that you tell me I will see the very sweet will of God. I will blindly obey." If only he had wished to discuss it! But no, he accepted everything, to the letter. Fortunate is the astuteness of the saints. I am sure that he gave his superiors more than one case of insomnia; it is not easy to be taken as delegates of the divine will. Therefore, knowing him to be so docile, so prompt to obey and so touchingly candid, everyone thought twice before contradicting him. Do you know, Father Maximilian, that you have been, in the main, and really without knowing it, a very great diplomat? We shall see later how this supernatural compliance was his invincible argument.

"And so," he continues, "with the permission of our Father Rector, on the eve of October 17, 1917, we held the first meeting of the first seven members: Father Joseph Pal, priest of the Roumanian province; Friar Anthony Glowinski, deacon of the Roumanian province, deceased in 1918; Friar Jerome Biasi of the Paduan province, deceased in 1929; Friar Quiricus Pignalberi, of the Roumanian province; Friar Anthony Mansi and Friar Henry Granata, both of the Neapolitan province; and myself.*

"This meeting took place in the evening secretly behind the closed doors of an inner cell. Before us was a statuette

---

*Though the first meeting was actually held the evening of October 16th, the liturgy for October 17th in those days had already begun—with the recitation of "First Vespers" of the Divine Office for the Feast of St. Margaret Mary Alacoque. Hence October 17th has always been celebrated as the anniversary day of the Militia's founding.—Ed.

of the Immaculata between two lighted blessed candles. Friar Jerome Biasi was secretary. We had in view the idea of establishing the program of the M.I., heartened by the promise of Father Alexander Basile, who was also the confessor of the Holy Father, that he would ask His Holiness to bless the M.I.

"However, Father Alexander did not keep his promise, and we obtained the Holy Father's verbal blessing through Bishop Dominic Jacquet of our Order, then professor of Church history in our college. For more than a year after the first meeting, the M.I. did not progress and so many obstacles arose that the members themselves did not dare to talk about it. One of them even tried to convince the others that all was absolutely useless. It was at that time that Friar Anthony Glowinski and, thirteen days later, Friar Anthony Mansi stricken with the Spanish grippe, died and went home to the Immaculata. As for me, I had a grave relapse; I was was coughing very much and spitting blood. Exempted from the courses, I took advantage of my time to recopy the program of the M.I. in order to be able to deliver it to the most Reverend Father General, Dominic Tavani, for his written blessing. As he wrote the blessing and expressed his desire to spread the M.I. among the Catholic youth, Father General remarked, 'If only there were twelve of you!'

"Since that day new members came in endlessly and in great numbers.

"During this first period, the activity of the M.I. consisted in praying and distributing the miraculous medal. Father General even gave us money to buy some."

May I be forgiven for extensively quoting this valuable text which certainly some day will become the object of even more important study. Before describing the work of Father Maximilian it is profitable to see its modest origin. God has certain methods which vary but little. At the bottom of every foundation, there is always much suffering, much contradiction, and much loneliness.

There were seven—"the seven sainted founders," Father Maximilian would say jokingly. But all seven did not believe equally in the future of the work. One of them, whom Father Maximilian charitably does not name, even tried to dissuade the others, saying that "none of them had much sense." The young religious did not have the right to defend his work, because Father General had forbidden him to be concerned about it.

"For more than a year," Father Pal writes in his testimony, "even with us, the first members of the Militia, he did not speak about his work." That was the year of the apparent apathy which he mentions. Others were talking of the work in order to undermine it, but he himself could say nothing. We can guess what that must have cost him!

It is significant that in his written statement Father Maximilian makes the impetus of his work coincide with the edifying deaths of two members of the Militia. "They went home to the Immaculata" simply to plead the cause of the knights devoted to her service. Father Maximilian never ceased to attach an extreme importance to his "heavenly reinforcements." One day he was to say, "Each time things are not going well, the Immaculata calls one of us to heaven that he may help us more efficaciously. Here below, we can work with only one hand, because with the other we must hold on to something in order not to fall ourselves; but in heaven, we will have our two hands free and the Blessed Virgin will be our Guardian."

Is there not in these words the freshness of the *Fioretti?*

I think that even to this day not enough has been made of the extremely delightful simplicity of Father Maximilian. A child's simplicity! He had been miraculously preserved from the damage of adult age, grief and sorrow, those bitter fruits of the failures of life, for let us note at once that Father Maximilian never suffered the least defeat. All that happened to him, absolutely ALL, came to him from the very gentle hands of his beloved Queen, who naturally gave him the best in the world. If he did not see it, did not understand—well, then, so much the better! In this way faith had the last word.

Since Saint Thérèse of the Infant Jesus, no one has done more to foster that childlike spirit which she helped us to recover and which is simply the ABC's of the gospel. *Nisi efficiamini sicut parvuli.** One could write a beautiful book on the charming candor of this bearded missionary, who often disconcerts us by his point-blank words, clear as the sword of the spirit and simple as heavenly logic. Only saints really take the trouble to draw all the conclusions of the translucent premise "God is love." Father Maximilian had remarkable good sense, and he was logical to the end.

---

*"Unless you become as little children" (Matthew 18, 13).

6

How to Win the Modern
World for Christ

How could he work so much with his continual headaches and his broken health? Not only did he pass all his
examinations, but he did so brilliantly, *summa cum laude*.
In 1915, he was already a doctor of philosophy, although
only twenty-one years of age. And he prepared with zeal for
examinations toward his doctorate in sacred theology, which
he passed four years later with the same success. I think that
this is one of the reasons why his superiors did not surmise
the gravity of his illness. A sick man does not succeed in all
his examinations with such ease, nor does he pass them as if
playing a game.

All his professors and all his fellow students agree in
crediting him with extraordinary abilities, even scientific
genius. Remarkable in everything, he excelled in mathematics
and continued to disconcert his most eminent professors.

"This boy," said Father Bondini, Rector of the College,
"asks me questions I cannot answer."

Father Leon Cicchito told me that there was no stopping
Friar Maximilian once he was carried off by enthusiasm and,
full of objections, passed from one problem to another by a
subtle chain of argument. After each solution he would bound
back with a new "Why?"

"While walking with me, he would not give me a rest but plied me with endless questions. A real bore," Father said with a laugh. But continuing very seriously, he added: "He was the most gifted youth with whom I had contact during the years of my rectorate. He had a *rare natural genius.*"

His mind was especially inclined to work out scientific discoveries. He was on the alert for any technical progress and was informed on all recent advances. One day, as reported by Father Eccher, Provincial of Padua, he drew the plans for an apparatus displaying extraordinary velocity. "He sketched the diagram with an expert hand, analyzed minutely all physico-mechanical laws which proved it, and charged me to present this scheme to Father Gianfranceschi, my professor at the Gregorian. He examined it with great attention and declared that according to the principles nothing argued against putting this daring theory into practice."

There is no doubt that this extraordinary young man devoted himself body and soul to his studies. Was he thinking, perhaps, that his talents would lead him to a scientific career? Why, no: his aims were essentially practical. Here, too, all the testimonies agree. As Father Pal, his schoolmate, sums it up, "He studied in order to refute the unbelievers."

From then on he faced them willingly and sometimes he provoked public discussions with strangers. Whether on the train or in the street, it was his preferred method of "hooking the fish." One day in Rome he encountered one of those "big fish," who was denouncing the Pope and the Church.

In the course of a close discussion, the unknown opponent exclaimed, "I know all about this, young fellow! I am a doctor of philosophy."

"And I also," replied the twenty-one-year-old friar who appeared to be sixteen.

The gentleman looked at him with amazement and abruptly changed his tone. (Well, one must be proper with colleagues!) Patiently, inexorably, the young doctor made him retreat, drove him to the wall. "At the end of the discussion," declares Father Pal, from whom we receive this delightful episode, "the unbeliever remained silent and seemed to meditate deeply."

This was Father Maximilian's method and he applied it often and with great success. Taken from boxing, it consisted in not allowing the opponent a chance to breathe, in pursuing him with pressing questions, apparently assuming his own position in order to defeat him on his own ground. "In order to do this," Father Maximilian thought with his clear mind, "I must be *on the alert.*" If it had depended only on him, Catholics would be everywhere and always the first in everything. When God allows him to ascend to the altars, he should be promoted as the patron of technicians and experts who fight on the front line to introduce Christ into the factories and laboratories.

Who, then, inspired this eminently modern spirit in him who, even as a student, was so much in advance of his own age? I have tried in vain to trace some connection. The courses he frequented seemed rather servilely faithful to outdated theories. One of his professors even defended the Ptolemaic system in the name of Saint Thomas. In this environment the spirit of Friar Maximilian appears to us doubly original and fresh, like the supernatural boldness which precisely characterized the Angelic Doctor in his time. What would have become of medieval philosophy if Saint Thomas and the other great Scholastics had shunned Aristotle as certain narrow-minded Catholics sulk at modern thought, condemning it in its entirety? "What is needed," Father Maximilian thought, "is to make all progress serve the glory of God, to *turn it into a weapon of conquest.*"

In his admirable allocution glorifying the virtues of Saint Joan of Lestonnac, Pope Pius XII extolled the extraordinary living interests of the saints that God brings to the altars. They are chosen from the crowd of the elect, the *turba magna,* because they fill the express need of our times and are to serve us as guides and masters *today*. But there are saints who seem to turn their back to their age. These elite souls stand aloof from the life of their times. Although heroes of virtue, they are fearful of progress. Friar Maximilian certainly did not figure among them. Joyously optimistic, he believed passionately that progress is good, provided it serves *ad maximam Dei gloriam*. It is necessary to take hold of progress and *give it meaning.*

We have been able to gather several characteristic episodes illustrating his way of seeing things, a way with which his companions did not always agree.

In 1917 the motion pictures were just making their appearance. They aroused suspicion in sound-thinking society, while the spellbound masses flocked to them. Most of the films were of very doubtful moral content and flattered the baser passions. The producers wanted one thing—to grow rich. It was wartime, the sad period when the arts and virtue slumber.

Evidently, at San Teodoro the motion pictures were often discussed. Certain professors plainly deplored this instrument of ruin. The films presented in Rome at that time were far from being a school of virtue. Friar Maximilian would listen, and his alert and independent spirit looked for a solution.

Suppress the movies? First of all, it was impossible. Then, too, would it be practical? Was it not more simple to transform them, to take possession of them and utilize them for good rather than permit them to serve evil?

One day he all but seriously shocked a somewhat conservative fellow student when, during a walk, the question arose. Friar Maximilian did not conceal his thought. "The screen can and must serve social welfare. It depends upon us to put it to the right use."

"Do you not see," exclaimed his companion, "that Satan and his agents take possession of all the inventions and all the achievements of progress to convert them to evil?"

"All the more reason to finally wake up and get to work in order to reconquer the positions taken by the enemy."

Time sided with the humble Franciscan friar. He could recall this conversation when Pope Pius XI officially authorized the movies as a means of the apostolate and an instrument of Catholic Action. So even the enthusiasts for the cinema should invoke him as patron!

But there is another even more effective weapon that Catholics should learn how to handle: it is the press, whose influence has grown steadily for a century. According to his Roman school friends, Friar Maximilian would often speak of it, both in common recreation and during the customary walks. From that time he dreamed of a magazine, under the spotless protection of the Immaculata, which would teach the gospel to all nations. The young friars would listen in astonishment and then, forgetting these dreams, return to their routine duties. But to Friar Maximilian they were not dreams! It was all a plan, a plan of battle.

In the midst of his brothers in religion he would at times feel peculiarly alone. None among them really understood him. Was it their fault? Surely not! How were they to measure themselves with this ardent soul, who could make his own the maxim of Saint Catherine of Siena, "My nature is fire"? He was a man of great, very great, desires, passionately enamored of universal conquest, consecrated by vocation to the "always more, always better." This it was that baffled his confreres and made his whole life a slow martyrdom. What can you do with a man who sees no limits to his desires and to his plans of conquest? Lacking the same inspiration and the same consuming love, how can you follow him without losing breath? It was not his fault that he was a saint! Surely the sanctifying Spirit ultimately granted him wings which he never failed to raise aloft, always aloft.

If the former classmates of Father Maximilan like to recount his intellectual feats, they actually relish the topic of his virtues. I perused these testimonies very attentively, but there are no stereotype expressions. These texts, which are written more or less awkwardly, all have the same tone of pure authenticity. To be sure, the adjectives flow freely—a common ailment in professional circles—but these appraisals serve only to set off the unanimous and persistent opinion.

All repeat to the point of monotony that they could find no fault in this man. They refer to certain former testimonies which prove that already very many considered him a saint. There were certain telling features in him. His observance was punctual: at the sound of the bell he was capable of abrupt silence in the midst of conversation with even a distinguished visitor; in the morning he would leap from bed at the first signal, although weak in health. His disposition was always the same, lively. His charity was fraternal. He spent hours in the aid of slow and less talented students who preferred to come to him because "no one knew how to explain things as clearly as he." His faithful obedience anticipated the least desires of his superiors. These are the traits which all emphasize with admiration.

"One day," relates Friar Albert Arzilli, his colleague at San Teodoro, "intending only to tease, I caused him considerable pain. Having obtained the necessary permission, I took him for a walk to show him a miraculous crucifix in one of Rome's churches. On the way he asked if I had obtained permission. At my seeming to have neglected that, he became disheartened and so intensely hurt that I quickly confessed in order to reassure him. Then he shook his handsome head with his characteristic gesture and smiled that innocent smile of his which was so appealing."

The testimonies concerning this period all agree in the praise of his apostolic zeal. He wanted, they say, to convert *all* sinners—*as fast as possible,* and in the entire world. For him sin was not an abstraction, for the thought of it hurt him to the bottom of his heart.

Father Pal tells us the following incident. "One day on coming back to the College from the Basilica of the Twelve Apostles, we met some rowdies who were blaspheming the Madonna. Friar Maximilian darted in among them and with tears in his eyes asked them why they hurt the Blessed Virgin so much. In confusion, they mumbled that they did so merely because they wanted to. Standing at a distance, I tried in vain to call back my friend. With his usual persistence, Friar Maximilian saw the thing through in order to convince these rascals that they were acting badly and must promise not to blaspheme any more. The ruffians, usually so nimble at answering back, stood silent and moved off as fast as possible."

On another occasion Friar Maximilian persuaded the same friend to accompany him to the Palazzo Verde, the offices of the Freemasons, to convert no less than the Grand Master himself! Encouraged by his friend's agreement, he went immediately to ask the Rector's permission. Imagine the expression on the Rector's face at such a proposal! Did he perhaps recall Saint Francis going to the land of the infidels to convert the high Sultan? Neither Friar Maximilian nor the Poverello had the least misgiving. In any case, Father Rector paternally told the young religious that he could request nothing better, but that it was perhaps expecting too much for the present—better to start praying for the conversion of the Freemasons. Friar Maximilian returned to his friend, a little sad and somewhat puzzled. He repeated the superior's answer and said, "Well, then, let's start to pray *right now."* That was Friar Maximilian indeed! Not tomorrow, not this evening, but right now. Not a single country, but the entire world!

This all-embracing love was a trait not especially commonplace among the Poles. Friar Maximilian loved his native country intensely. We know how much he suffered when, one day at the College, they took him for a German. One could even say that this loyalty was the remote cause of his death. Had they not proposed to him before his imprisonment that he pass himself off as a Pole of German origin? Many others had done so and were not necessarily traitors, for they often used their papers of authorization to help their countrymen. Father Maximilian stubbornly refused the least compromise with this plan. He wanted to live and die a Pole.

It was very different, however, when it was a question of the Church of Christ, in which one was "neither Greek nor Jew." His plans of conquest did not stop at any frontier, at any barrier. They were as all-embracing as the Church. Here was something that puzzled some of his countrymen: how could he openly declare that he loved even the Germans? And yet it was true. He loved them in Christ, as children of the Immaculata—although sometimes ungrateful children. This is the charity that admits no exception and is the touchstone of our Christianity.

It was he, the humble Franciscan religious, whose vision was truly correct, even from his Polish viewpoint! For true patriotism, which is at opposite poles with exaggerated nationalism, will not contradict the law of Christ. It often figures among those things added in good measure to those who loyally seek first the kingdom of God. Temporal kingdoms have nothing to lose in glorifying their saints, who with catholic hearts crave the souls of *all.*

In April, 1918, the war was approaching its end. On the twenty-eighth, in the full exultation of a Roman spring, Friar

Maximilian was ordained priest. The next day, he celebrated his first Mass at the altar of Sant' Andrea delle Fratte, where the commemorative plate reads: "In 1842 the Blessed Virgin appeared to the Hebrew Ratisbonne in order to transform this fierce wolf into a gentle lamb." With soul overwhelmed by an inexpressible joy, he pronounced alone for the first time the words of Consecration. Here he was, in a certain sense, the master of the Precious Body and Blood, the dispenser of the mercy of God—at last, armed for boundless conquest! From above the altar, the Warrior Queen seemed to smile at him; he knelt down and would lock up in his overflowing heart the entire world. He was ready.

A year later the war ended, and his superiors in Poland recalled him. He left equipped with two doctorates, but his heart held still greater riches. "Woe betide knowledge which does not turn to love," says Bossuet in a memorable sermon. Father Maximilian learned much in Rome, but it was in the science of the saints that he acquired his most glorious diplomas. He felt himself being entirely consumed in the living flame of love of which he willingly made himself both the glory and the prey.

In one of his last letters to his mother, we read: "Pray for me, Mother, so that my love may grow more and more quickly and without any limit. *Pray especially that it will be without limits.*" And this last sentence he underlines.

The great desire of the young religious will be granted. He will always be—even in his death—the man "without limits."

7

"No Prophet is Acceptable in His Own Country"

He returned to Poland in July, 1919, worn by tuberculosis—"so far gone," testifies Father Kubit, Guardian of Niepokalanow, "that the doctors gave him at most three months to live."

His case was clear. However, he was assigned to the Franciscan friary at Cracow, where the climate is fatal to tuberculars. What to do with this man who is so sick? It is very simple: they made him a professor.

Some could be shocked at this, even accuse the superiors of unbelievable imprudence. It is easy to pass judgment, looking down and from a distance! But it was 1919, when after four years of war Poland, finally free, was bled white. The economic situation was disastrous, the treasury empty. Private donations, family souvenirs, and numerous alliances provided the first recovery funds of the national treasury. But these heroic sacrifices did not prevent the catastrophe. A drastic devaluation of currency threatened to ruin the country. In 1914, one could buy a two-story house for the price of two pounds of bacon today. And then a new storm approached from the East. The Red army launched upon its conquest of Europe. Does the world not remember that Poland, singlehanded, checked for twenty years the imperialistic designs of Moscow?

"The miracle of the Vistula" decided the destiny of Europe. But the country, though saved in the moment of death, was ravaged, its suffering unspeakable. Devastating epidemics spread in the provinces of the East, which had been the most unfortunate. Priests and religious killed themselves with work. Was this the time to think of one's self? One must hold on until the end and, if necessary, leap into the breach, as a good soldier. No, the superiors of Father Maximilian should not be condemned for not sparing him at this time of extreme distress, even though it would have been done if they had known. After all, was he not one sick person who *never* complained? Besides, they needed professors. In Poland during those four years of war their ranks grew light, and this zealous young friar ravaged by the fever which gave him those beautiful red cheeks was only too "available"!

Not only was his body exhausted by work, but his soul was harrowed by ridicule. He had hoped on returning to interest all the friars of the Cracow friary in his work—not really his work but that of his Immaculata. Instead they shrugged their shoulders. They listened to him with light smiles of pity, then laughed among themselves, calling him a bore and a dreamer: "Behold! the dreamer cometh."

They found an even better nickname, one which was to cling to him for a long time, "Marmelade." When they saw him approaching, they would whisper among themselves, "Look, it's animated marmelade!" The young priest walked very slowly, breathing with difficulty to avoid any abrupt movement which could provoke hemorrhage. He who was by nature of a quick temperament became very patient and proverbially mild. And so the nickname originated. One witness, a layman, recalls an occasion when a member of the community mocked Father Maximilian before his face, showing him how he moved so slowly at the altar during Mass.

Imitating Father Maximilian's gestures, he commented, "Such marmelade!"

Although the poor priest said nothing, he suffered keenly. This bitter experience was not fruitless, for he later displayed an unbounded tenderness and sweetness to the sick. On this subject I gathered more than one touching testimony. Even when the coffers of the friary were half empty, the beloved sick wanted for nothing. He had an infinite indulgence for their whims. "Better than a mother," one friar told me with tears in his eyes. "You must put yourself in their place," the priest would say to the hospital attendants. *"You must understand them."* And he would himself treat them as his best fellow workers.

It was not only his cautious movements that provoked laughter and criticism; he was resented *because he was different from the others.* All saints are victims of this same resentment. They enter into our quiet little lives like a walking stick thrust into an ant's nest. Without willing it and often without knowing it, they compel us to make certain rather unpleasant examinations of conscience.

We learn to make certain adjustments with the vow of poverty: Well, what are "mental reservations" good for anyway? Then along comes this "Marmelade" to upset you with his outmoded observance. You smoke. Is it a sin to smoke? Why, no! You have even the permission of your superiors. But in the twinkling of an eye he forces you to calculate how much money you send up in smoke each year, and all that could have been done with that money. Even though he says nothing, he has a certain way of looking at you, a candid and penetrating gaze which makes you feel uneasy. A walking rebuke! What have we left with which to defend ourselves except the dread weapon of ridicule?

The fact is that at Cracow they treated him as though he were harmlessly insane or at best a poor fool. One day at

Grodno, when his work was at its peak, a confrere came to look around. Unable to control his astonishment, he crudely blurted out before the friars: "And to think that as a student he was so hidebound, so impractical!" Father Maximilian blushed but controlled himself and said nothing. Did he think then of the words of Saint Paul, *"We are fools for Christ"?** He valued his academic titles and his intelligence only insofar as they could help win souls, never to shine before others. He let people say and do as they wished. A great many of his brothers did not believe in him, and some will believe only when he ascends to the altars.

As was to be expected, about the end of 1919 he had a serious relapse. The fever climbed to 105 degrees. Our witness for this period is Friar Bombrys, who lived in the same friary. He tells us that, fearing contagion, no one went to see Father Maximilian. We owe to the same witness the description of the poverty of Father Maximilian's cell.

"There was a cupboard and an old truckle-bed with a straw mattress so worn that it sank down like a cradle. On the cupboard at the foot of the bed there was a statue of the Immaculata. Images of the recently beatified Gemma Galgani and Thérèse of the Child Jesus stood on the old desk in the corner."

He became so weak that they finally sent him to the sanatorium at Zakopane. He remained there from August 10, 1920 until April 29, 1921. From Zakopane he went to the sanatorium at Nieszaw where he was treated from May 4 to November 3, 1921. It was a time of apostolate through suffering, but also of direct action. He quickly sized up the situation. Some sections of the sanatorium at Zakopane were completely deprived of religious assistance and directed by persons hostile to the clergy. The rest house reserved for uni-

---

*I Corinthians 4, 10.

versity people appeared to be a real bastion of unbelief. One fine day, Father Maximilian put a handful of "shells" or "bullets" in his pocket, looked with infinite love at the statue of the Immaculata, and took advantage of a walk to engage in battle.

There was only one practicing Catholic in this sanatorium, which was occupied by intellectuals. From her we have an animated report of every phase of the "campaign." First of all, he had a trait that we shall notice more than once. The young priest had a really irresistible charm; a single look, a smile could win a heart completely. He did so well that the students invited him to give lectures to while away the boring hours at the sanatorium. Well, he was just waiting for that.

Bedridden, that single Catholic student was unable to attend his lectures. She had her comrades give her all the details. All agreed that the young priest was unusually intelligent and extremely erudite. He had a gift of convincing those who preferred not to be convinced and who therefore would not venture into his presence.

"He knew how to say the proper thing to each one; he possessed a real talent for reaching unbelievers."

Soon after his arrival, he caused a great stir by converting four notorious freethinkers. Very many others went to confession. Among the most assiduous at the conferences was a young Jewish medical student of Tarnow. He grew more and more ill and one day told Father Maximilian that he was no doubt attending his last conference. The priest consoled him, saying that he would come to see him. However, access to the critical cases was forbidden. Even so, this specialist of the impossible gained admittance. Informed in time, Father Maximilian went to the dying young man, who asked for baptism and the last rites. The priest then hung the miraculous medal around his neck. The dying man was in raptures, but a single thought sullied his happiness: he feared the arrival of his mother, a formidable woman, fiercely dedicated to her religion.

"Set your mind at ease, my son; you will be in heaven before that."

He died very peacefully at eleven o'clock, and his mother came at twelve. With a shriek she tore the miraculous medal from his neck. The sanatorium resounded with her screams.

"You have killed my son! You have stolen my son from me!"

There was a great scandal. The director of the sanatorium was very much upset over it and notified Father Maximilian to leave and not enter again. How little he knew this priest!

"The Immaculata gave me the strength to resist," Father Maximilian wrote to his brother, "and I answered that at visiting hours I could come the same as everyone else."

He returned and did so well that other conversions followed. There was a complete series of apologetical talks from the existence of God to the divinity of Christ. Gentle as lambs, the unbelievers of yesterday obtained New Testaments and other background books recommended by Father Maximilian and started to study conscientiously. This demon of a man was not stopping halfway.

Well-tried tenacity was a salient trait of his character. When he was sure of his facts, he never yielded. Chased through the door, he would return to do battle through the window. We could quote more than one delightful incident. One day, he had fixed his choice on a Protestant pastor of Nieszawa. He drove him so relentlessly into a corner that the terrified pastor blocked up the door against him. What a surprise when he saw Father Maximilian reappear through the back stairs, calmly declaring, "I would like to take up again your objections of the other day. Since the text of Saint

Matthew on the Supremacy of Peter is not an interpolation, then . . . "

"What a bore!" Father Cicchito had told me as he recalled with a smile the eternal "Why?" of the young student. "What bad luck!" the Protestant pastor unquestionably thought. Father Maximilian was a dangerous adversary, who did not let go his hold; and when he tracked down a soul, you can be sure that in the end he would bring it back to the Good Shepherd, like a sheepdog in quest of lambs lost in the woods.

At Zakopane, he worked only within the limits set by holy obedience, following strictly the prescribed treatment. He therefore had ample time to pray during the long hours spent on the couch. He made suffering his trade and he did it well!

In the letters to his brother, which are real jewels, his ardent soul clearly appears to be craving the "always more."

"I am delighted with what you have written me, and if you fulfill all your resolutions you will soon be a saint. But it is a road to which there is no end. *Qui sanctus est, sanctificetur adhuc*[*]—the saint must *continue* to sanctify himself. The more we engage ourselves on the way of sanctity, the more we realize how little we have accomplished compared to what remains to be done. The faster we run, the more we realize the slowness of the race. With the dying Saint Francis we must say, 'Let us *begin* to do good . . . ' "

He might have been taken for an experienced spiritual director, but he was only twenty-six. He certainly did not preach a life of convenience, and he knew how to strike a telling blow.

"Your letters make a strange impression on me," his brother responded. "When I talk with others of the ideals of

_____
[*]Apocalypse 22, 11.

the priesthood, it seems to me that I am very far advanced. But a letter from you is enough to make me see myself where I really am—at the bottom of the ladder. I feel a sort of deception; it is my pride that revolts. Then I humble myself and I get down to work." This was delightful candor on the part of the one who liked to call himself Brother Leo and whose whole ambition until death was only to follow step by step this new Poverello.

We have other letters of this period addressed to Father Maximilian. They express more than a treatise in psychology.

In looking them over, in spite of myself I thought of the famous door of the Baptistery of Saint John Lateran. When the sexton very proudly makes it turn on its hinges, he invariably says, "It is not surprising; *there is silver in it.*"

Well, may the Lord forgive me, but in most of the letters from his confreres I do not hear the unique ring which says, "There is silver here." These confreres appear to be—I would not dare to say that they are—prodigiously uninspired. Accustomed to mediocrity, they see only their little personal routines, suspicious of all "exaggeration"—and of all heroism. They ask only one thing: to live peacefully.

The exceptional letters are the nine of Father Venance, who died in the odor of sanctity January 31, 1921. These pages scribbled in haste by a dying man do have the unique ring of silver, the incomparable voice of the Holy Spirit. These two friars had seen each other only a few times, but their souls recognized each other as kindred. "I do not know how to explain it," writes Father Venance, "but from the first day my heart has been filled with a very great affection for you, and it has seemed to me that we share the same ideals and the same eagerness, although you surpass me in intelligence and your progress in perfection."

This dying Franciscan was the best ally of Father Maximilian. Until the end, he encouraged him with letters of fresh life and incomparable humility. He did even more from beyond, "where he could work with both hands"!

Admirable is the pact of the saints, who, from heaven to earth, from earth to heaven, do not cease to plot together, to help each other.

8

Implementing the M.I.'s
War Plan

Seven had engaged themselves under the banner of the Immaculata on that memorable eve of October 17, 1917. Two had meanwhile died the death of the elect. The others?

I dare say that only Father Maximilian, the leader of the group, interpreted his consecration to the letter, totally, absolutely and irrevocably. Certainly this is not an unkind criticism of the others, for we can safely affirm that there were holy men among them. But they had not the ample, ardent inspiration and—let us say the word—the *genius* of the young Polish friar.

When he left Rome, he ran the risk that his ideas become anchored within the limits of a small, devout confraternity. Father Maximilian had not wanted that when he founded the Militia of the Immaculata!

We cannot refrain from repeating, even to the point of tiring, that he was a man of very great desires, literally consumed by a thirst for souls, having as his objective the whole world. Nothing less than *all* could satisfy him. This point was such a distinctive feature of his character that all his thoughts, his plans and his works have meaning only under the light of this imposing vision. He would never say "save *some* souls," but "save *all* souls." And lest one risked being mistaken in giving these words a merely spatial sense, he never failed to add: "those which are now on earth, and those which will be on earth, even until the end of time." I think that the word *all* is the one word which recurred most often in his vocabulary, and this is undoubtedly true concerning his letters. Such ambitions could be the exploits of only a fool—or of a saint. It is not surprising that some may have taken him for a feeble-minded person. At that time, his great desires had not yet undergone the test of time. The future was needed to prove his case.

But there was more to it. One might describe the saints as implacable realists, who give words their simplest and most ordinary sense, their fullest import and weight. They say nothing, they promise nothing carelessly. They tremble before the fathomless depths of certain expressions which appear dull and ordinary to us. Unaware of being poets and great masters of the word, they restore to language all its lost nobility. In their delicate hands the most humble, the most ordinary things become a hymn of glory: Sister Water and Brother Fire, Sister Dove and even Brother Wolf. If these creatures obey them, is it not because they recognize their *proper names?*

In the same way, every promise they make is equivalent to an oath. To it they give themselves entirely, fulfilling its very last letter. How many good souls have repeated day after day, according to the example of the Little Flower, the consecration of self to the Infinite Love? But exceptionally rare are they who fully understand what they say, who know *where* this will lead them if God takes them at their word.

Now, there were seven who made promises in that inner cell at San Teodoro, but I think that only Father Maximilian knew what he was saying and what he was taking upon himself.

What was his chief idea? In short, what did he want? To conquer ALL souls for Christ, in the WHOLE world, until the end of time, through the Immaculata. Nothing more, nor less.

But who wills an objective also wills the means to it. Here, too, we see his inexorable logic and very solid theology. Since the Immaculata is the "Mother of all grace," giving us Christ the Saviour, since she is the dispenser of the gift of God and the official delegate of His mercy, it suffices to surrender one's self unconditionally to her gentle guidance in order that, having become her docile instruments, we may accomplish wonders.

We read these lines and they appear sound and perfectly orthodox. But to take it up from there. *literally* to *incarnate* them, in a word to live them, is as far as one can go. We all say the Our Father, but some of the saints, fascinated by the first words, could continue no further. The entire doctrine of Father Maximilian is contained in these few lines, but they suffice for him to undertake the conquest of the world.

He had no desire to establish a devout confraternity, although his Militia had obtained the official title of "Pious Union." He did not even wish to limit his Militia to the Franciscan Order, although he felt throughout his life a justifiable pride that it had begun there. His vision was as broad as the Church! Through its consecration to the Immaculata, the Militia must radiate to all religious Congregations, to all Orders, and to all the works of Catholic Action, because its purpose and *raison d'être* consisted in completing and bringing to the supreme splendor of holiness every vocation, whatever it be. Thus, far from being narrow, it was directed toward fullness. The efficacious means for attaining this was the act of consecration to the Immaculata, to be embodied, lived, accepted down to the last letter. One will understand nothing of Father Maximilian if one does not understand this keystone of all his work.

But there is yet another trait that we cannot stress too much. All his biographers are in accord in extolling his abundant activity. He was, as Americans would say, a giant of efficiency. Someone has written with good reason that his work has been his greatest miracle. But I know no one who was less an "activist" than he. If the scholastic definition which describes the apostolate as an overflow of the interior life, *superabundantia contemplationis,* ever needed to be proved by example, this life, wonderful in every respect, would be sufficient to confirm it. Father Maximilian always defended the primacy of the spiritual and did not cease to put his sons and disciples on guard against the most subtle of heresies, that of "activism."

In the program of the M.I he points out four means which the knight of Our Lady must employ: the living witness of one's own life, prayer, suffering and work. He will not cease to repeat (*Experto crede!*—believe one who knows from experience!) that we gain more through suffering than through direct action. The work of the Immaculata must be a flowering of the interior life, brisk water that overflows, and flame that mounts—*Bonum diffusivum sui**; otherwise, it will be but a caricature and, worse than that, a treason. Father Maximilian never contradicted this fundamental thought. Never did the wine of success go to his head. What he said now, he was to say twenty years later when the City of the Immaculata became a humming beehive of intense work. To compromise the primacy of the spiritual would be to compromise all his work.

But, to come to the point, how did his work commence? The perplexed reader sees no connection between the be-

---

*The good tends to impart itself.

ginning of this chapter and this invalid, on whom the doctors were prepared to do a pneumothorax, the other lung being also infected. Now it is time to tell that, before leaving for the sanatorium, Father Maximilian had cast to the ground his little grain of mustard seed. It was so small and so insignificant that no one took him seriously and some were even chuckling over it.

So he established at Cracow his first Militia circle. Of course, he proposed it first to his confreres, but with little success. Then he turned to the "Gentiles," as he liked to call the lay people. Once a month, meetings took place in the so-called Italian Room near the friary of the Franciscan Fathers. The number of candidates increased daily. People were attracted by this young religious with a childlike face, who smiled when he spoke of his "heavenly Mother" and seemed enraptured in serving her. He preached more by his mere presence than by his word.

We have from this period a single conference addressed to the clerics, dated November 15, 1919. It is a text in every respect revealing, a text well worth translating in its entirety. One note dominates throughout: the praise of suffering, that fire "in which all gold is purified." He speaks of it with the inimitable accent that only experience can lend. Certain passages are so lucid that one hardly dares to read between the lines for fear of learning things meant to be concealed. He knows persecution and excuses it as part of the program. "Sometimes," he says, "our best intentions are misinterpreted; and some go even so far as to calumniate us. These persecutions come not only from enemies, but also from good and pious persons, even saints, perhaps even from some registered in the files of the M.I.

"There is no greater sorrow than to see how these persons obstruct every road, desiring thereby only the glory of God as they exert themselves to destroy what we have built and to alienate other souls from us.

"Well, if everything is against us, what remains to us as a lighthouse and compass?"

The answer is clear and undeniable: "holy obedience," by which the will of the Immaculata is manifested. My superiors can make mistakes; I make no mistake in obeying them. "If today obedience tells me 'yes,' I will do it; if tomorrow it says 'no,' I will not do it—and I will never say that I made a mistake." He, in obeying, could not be mistaken; but his superiors . . . ? Seeing him so docile, did they not feel a sort of uneasiness?

Above all, it is not to be thought that in finding himself so contradicted, so opposed, he felt the least bitterness. There are certain holy souls who wear their martyr's crown very much in evidence. But not he—not in the least. And it is with joy, with a very pure Franciscan joy, that he welcomed "his Sister Suffering."

"All these trials," he says, "are very useful, necessary, and even indispensable, like the crucible where gold is purified."

Not only useful, but desirable. "When grace inflames our hearts, it stirs up a real thirst for suffering, the ability to suffer without limits, to be despised, humiliated. Our suffering testifies as to how much we love our Father in heaven and our beloved Mother, the Immaculata. Because suffering is the only school of love."

There is no need to be told that he had passed his grades at the school where one learns the science of saints, the science of the Cross!

"We will do very much more," he goes on, "if we are plunged into exterior and interior darkness, filled with sorrow, weakened, exhausted, without consolation, persecuted at each step, surrounded by continual failures, abandoned by all, ridiculed, scoffed at as was Jesus on the Cross; provided that we pray with all our strength for those who persecute us, and provided that we want by all means to draw them to God, through the Immaculata . . . " Above all, the objective is "to desire, and desire without limits."

"After our death, the Immaculata will complete our work. Then we will be able to do much more than we do on this poor earth, where, in holding out our hand to others, we must be so careful not to fall ourselves. We must not grieve if we do not see here below the fruits of our works; perhaps it is the will of God that we gather them after our death."

Let us remember that the young friar who spoke thus, as a master, was only twenty-five. Although consumed by fever, he leaped to the attack within the month. A soul of such mettle was made for great achievements.

* * *

The apostolate of sickness had lasted long enough. Although not cured, he felt better and his superiors allowed him to return to Cracow and resume his work. He now began the new phase so long desired. The membership of the M.I. flourished so well that the Italian Room could no longer accommodate them. Moreover, very many who lived in the suburbs complained that they could not attend the meetings. A centralized meeting-place had to be obtained as soon as possible; and there was need of a modest bulletin or at least an inexpensive circular.

The superiors could see no reason to disapprove. "On the condition," they said, "that you can raise the funds. Your friary is too poor to furnish the money." If they expected to discouraged him by refusing the means, they certainly did not know him very well. For love of his Immaculata, Father Maximilian was determined to *beg*.

He later confessed how painful this was. Before knocking at the first door, he turned back three times. Three times

76

he violently forced himself to return. Finally, with extreme reluctance and blushing in shame, he asked for money toward this uncertain and unfeasible project. A charitable priest of Cracow was his first fortunate victim. These few alms and the subscriptions of the members of the M.I., who were almost all very poor, defrayed the expenses of the first issue of the bulletin. It appeared in the month of January, in 1922, at the height of the crisis, when the most solidly established reviews were falling off. Humbly, unpretentiously, without acclaim and without a cover, it made its first appearance with this word of apology "from the editors"; "Because of lack of funds, we cannot guarantee our readers regular delivery of the review."

It had a significant title: *The Knight of the Immaculata*. The poor priest had no assistants. He had to write the first number practically alone. Furthermore, he was gifted with no special literary talent in the ordinary sense of the term. He had better than that: a transparently clear style, a flair for the right word, a holy zeal that spread to everyone. What mattered all the obstacles! He went ahead.

The second number was sent to press. Meanwhile, devaluation was running its course; when time came to pay the printer, he had not a penny. The Guardian of the friary had expected just this. Shrugging his shoulders, he quoted a Polish proverb. "This is what happens, my son, when you try to attack the moon with a spade. It is now your affair to clear yourself—without jeopardizing the friary!"

Then the Immaculata intervened directly. After Mass, the poor editor in distress found on the altar of the Blessed Virgin an envelope containing money, the exact amount of the printing bill. A clumsy hand had written, "For my dear Mother, the Immaculata." Without a moment's delay he ran to his superior. There was general astonishment. The so-called coincidence was too striking to bear discussion; Father

Maximilian had permission to dispose of the money—which he did.

The growth of the little blue magazine was thereafter an uninterrupted miracle. Even if there were not so many spectacular coincidences, numberless facts combined to indicate the more or less direct intervention of Divine Providence. With characteristically vivid faith, Father Maximilian put in the bottom of the worthless cardboard box that he was using as cash-box a picture of Blessed Joseph Benedict Cottolengo and named him his cashier. It was well for him that he did so, for the founder of the "Piccola Casa" did not find himself out of his element. In this hectic business of editing they thought only of maximum output for today, never of tomorrow. Providence was taking care of tomorrow for them.

Someone who knew him very well told me: "There are in the life of Father Maximilian two miracles that should be sufficient to canonize him. First, his health. He had only one quarter of a lung! Then, his work. Starting from nothing, it flourished contrary to all the expectations of so-called common sense. No one ever completely understood it, not excluding Father Maximilian himself. Moreover, he was satisfied that the Immaculata, and she alone, keep the secret."

His confreres did not encourage him at all. To them this rash enterprise seemed proof enough that the good Father Maximilian was a little deranged. Some were even openly hostile. One of them exclaimed that their holy founder, Saint Francis, intended them to preach and hear confessions, not publish magazines.

Such objections face ready rebuttal. Did Saint Francis travel by train, by automobile or airplane? Were there printing establishments in his time? Good logic should prompt the exclusion of all newspapers and reviews from the friary. But no, there is no need to rest in the thirteenth century as in a comfortable armchair.

Father Maximilian, however, said none of these things. He let the storm pass, then went to ask his superior's approval of another proposal. This time it was not a trifling request. He needed a printing press, because changing printers five times within a year had nearly proved disastrous. The press was an old model, but that mattered little.

Father Provincial answered as usual. "I allow it, on the sole condition that you find the money."

Since Father Maximilian had not a farthing, how could it be done? As always, he paid with his person. If saints accomplish the miraculous, we do not generally know what it costs them!

Visiting the friary at Cracow was an American priest recently arrived to view the rehabilitation of Poland. During recreation, some decided to amuse the visitor at the expense of the poor editor. They began by criticizing his review for poor presentation and inferior contents. Another laughingly pointed out Father Maximilian as the priest whose plan it was to conquer the whole world. A third in mock confidence revealed that this poor simple priest was dreaming of setting up his own print shop. What a pity that he had so few pennies and so many debts!

Father Maximilian said not a word in self-defense and showed no slightest sign of anger. Humiliated, he cast his eyes down and covered his mouth with a silencing hand. We can envision him with that characteristic movement of his head, externally calm but cut to the quick. His hand over his mouth made doubly sure that no impatient word escaped.

The American Father showed his distaste for these jokes. These so-called wild ideas of Father Maximilian, far from shocking him, helped him formulate his opinion, coming from the United States as he did. The young priest wanted to buy a printing press? Why, he might have wanted that himself! Quietly but cooly, he spoke.

"My dear Fathers, instead of making fun of him, would it not be better to help him pay for the machine?"

Then in the midst of a frozen silence, he turned to Father Maximilian, who was now more confused than ever. "As a start, here is a small donation." On the spot he wrote a check for a hundred dollars—at that time, a small fortune.

So it was that Father Maximilian was able to buy an old printing machine from the Sisters of Divine Mercy at Lagiewniki near Cracow. This was the same community of Sisters in which another little saint was maturing in sanctity, Sister Faustina, the apostle of Infinite Love.

It became clear that this apostolate of the press was incompatible with that already assigned to the Cracow friary. The fervent editor had to inject a new routine within that already existing in the community. Moreover, the noisy stir had become intolerable to the aged friars who had been retired to that friary. The poor old men were exhausted. Finally, the superiors had come to dread Father Maximilian's next request. These requests for permission set them up as arbiters of holy obedience, as the consecrated spokesmen of the wishes of the Immaculata—a difficult situation, indeed! A solution was unavoidable; they had to look about for a place that would take him in.

Then the idea struck. They would send him to Grodno, at the other end of Poland. The building was already falling into ruin, and certainly they couldn't be criticized for sending him there. With complete honesty they could recommend the healthful climate of this old oriental city, today in full decline. So the poor knight of the Immaculata would find himself in the wilderness; but, at least, those in Cracow could breathe more easily.

How many times will we overhear in Father Maximilian's letters his sad complaint, "Oh, Cracow! Oh, Cracow!" Only God knows how much he suffered there. He suffered in his body and in his soul; but the affliction of soul was gain. This expression of anguish was wrenched from him, not indeed because of his own sufferings: he was tormented by the thought of some souls dedicated to perfection being engulfed little by little in a life of mediocrity. He suffered so because he envisioned the cause of God at stake.

9

Grodno—Or the Secret of the Miraculous Draught of Fishes

Saints have a certain way of working wonders which we overlook through our nearsightedness. Their arithmetic is very simple: they do all they can, more than they can, spending themselves without counting the cost; and when they reach the limits of their strength, they say: "Now, Lord, it is Your turn, because I am at the very end of my means." Is this not their way of driving a bargain with Infinite Love?

Father Maximilian, who knew all the tricks of the saints, engaged himself in his wild enterprise of universal conquest *with nothing* to his credit, not even health. He asked but one thing: namely, to use even to the end of his tether the little strength left him. Each instant of his life and each drop of his blood he converted into a holocaust and then *let the Immaculata act.* "Mother, I have done all I can; you will do your part and do it well!" Would not the all-beautiful and the all-good Queen be taken at her word?

One day during his illness, he asked the friars to put his glasses and his watch at the foot of the Immaculata's statue. They thought he was delirious. Then he smilingly explained, "My glasses are my eyes, my thought, my work. The watch is the time that I have left. All this belongs to her, to her alone. It does not belong to me any longer. I have given all to her. Then, is it not proper that she use it as she pleases?"

His sole desire was to be an instrument in her mighty hands. He became just that and learned very quickly the art of making his nothingness bear fruit, because nothing pleases the Blessed Virgin more than poverty of means.

At Grodno, the city with a glorious past but now fully in ruin, he was helped by her to his heart's content. His only springboard was his superiors' authorization to start from zero. As assistants, he was given a lay brother and a brother-candidate. The former, Friar Albert Olzakowski, was literally to die from overwork in this loving exploit. Later, Father Maximilian would often invoke him as numbered among his heavenly reinforcements.

When he arrived at Grodno on October 20, 1922, the friary was a shambles. They let him do as he wished, but he found among the very aged friars retired there neither support nor understanding. Only the good Father Fordon, Guardian of the friary, allowed himself to be gradually won to the cause. In the end, he proved to be a priceless help: for he too, an invalid tubercular, went to join "the troops in heaven" that he might work hard there for the cause.

The house was large and three rooms could be assigned to the use of the unpretentious little periodical. The first sheltered the administration; the second was called the print shop; the third was assigned to the shipping. The editing office was in the cell of Father Maximilian, the floor of which was heaped with newspapers and reviews, for there were neither shelves nor closets.

They called the machine bought with the hundred dollars "old Grandmother." It took no less than all one's might to operate it. Sixty thousand turns were required to print five thousand copies, the circulation at that time. All the personnel worked from morning until night—and often from night until morning. It was an exhausting and very unhealthy work, for it demanded an almost uninterrupted bending position.

We have the memoirs of one of the friars who confesses that, although he was very young at that time, he was sometimes worn out and every minute seemed an hour to him.

Father Maximilian worked as the others, even more than the others since he was not exempt from either the breviary or any of the conventual obligations. He heard confessions just as the other Fathers, often for hours on end. He did penance for his so-called journalistic "sins" by performing punctually all his other duties. He was often sent on sick calls to distant villages and would not return until night, exhausted by many miles of travel in a wretched cart. The brothers likewise could not attend to the printing until they had finished the duties of the house. They cleaned, cut wood, and did the housework in the priests' quarters. The food at that time was absolutely insufficient. The cash-box of the friary was often empty, but for nothing in the world would the brave little group draw money from the Immaculata to buy a few extras. The money from the review served for only one thing: to increase the printing, to build up the stock of tools. The laborers did not count!

We ought not to picture Father Maximilian as a merciless boss, stingy with wages and thinking only of production. He would curb the friars; but, transported with holy enthusiasm, they continually begged him not to spare them, since they also wanted to spend themselves for love of the Blessed Virgin. The true story of these marvelous beginnings shows Father Maximilian as a splendid trainer. He preached only through example, but *that was sufficient,* for heroism is contagious. Is it not sometimes only the first step that hurts? The little board of editors lived for years, almost without realizing it, in an atmosphere of heroism.

Soon afterward, another brother came, bringing with him a hidden fear; in sending him, the Provincial had informed him that he was going to work with the worst taskmaster who ever existed. It is to him, Brother Gabriel, that we owe these touching memories.

The five thousand copies of the printing were quickly distributed; but devaluation continued to slump, and wages grew more meager. This, however, mattered but little because hand labor cost nothing and the little group had only one ambition, to increase the circulation.

Every few months, when subscriptions increased, the brothers went in a delegation to the editor-priest to ask his permission to take on a little more work. The good Father, moved to tears, protested feebly and then wrote to Father Provincial asking his authorization of an increase in the printing. One of the elated friars ran to mail the letter. Three days later Father Maximilian announced the good news: "Well, my sons, go to work!" Then they took a few more hours from their much needed sleep for the extra work and at night had a little worse backache and a little more blood on their fingers.

Father Maximilian not only labored himself as a simple workman treading for hours the pedal of the machine and turning the famous wheel but he also furnished almost all the articles. These he wrote hastily "during leisure moments," he says, which means late at night. Sometimes he had to write them as fast as the brothers could print them. The assistant writers were few and mediocre. The success of the review, then, must be attributed to him almost exclusively.

Repetition must emphasize the fact that he had none of the style of current journalism. The striking element in his articles is their logic and their simplicity. Father Maximilian plies his premises to their conclusion, hedging in his readers until they are obliged to declare themselves. But the secret of his success is the inner flame that consumed him and his boundless, inexpressible love for the Immaculata. Are not all lovers poets at times? When he begins to speak of her, he instinctively finds words trembling and aflame with the deepest feeling.

The fact is that at a time when devaluation brought bankruptcy to important reviews, *The Knight of the Immaculata* increased its circulation from month to month. In spite of their best intention, it was impossible for the poor friars to satisfy the demand. Enthusiastic readers were asking for back issues, and when the supply of these was exhausted they begged for only the loan of reserve copies in order to recopy them.

Most of the readers of the review were very ordinary people. Father Maximilian was writing, not for academic centers, but for the masses. It is remarkable that this young religious holding two doctorates and considered by his professors as an embryonic genius adapted himself to the needs of the people and possessed an uncommon gift of clearness. His short apologetical articles in dialogue form are truly exemplary in their class. In an attractive form *The Knight of the Immaculata* was presenting doctrine, recalling catechism, redirecting and deepening devotion to the Blessed Virgin. This devotion had always been a favorite of the Polish people, and Father Maximilian was now preparing to climax it by total consecration to the Immaculata, for this was the ultimate objective of the Militia.

What was the financial standing of this now steadily growing review? I answer unhesitatingly that the kingdom of God was sought *before all else,* with an absolute confidence that all the rest would be superadded without fail. We may say that the saint is a walking provocation, a real challenge thrown to God: "Lord, You have promised much. Now I take You at Your word. You must comply!"

At first they sent the review *gratis* to anyone who asked for it. You can be sure that everyone was eager to receive these free subscriptions! Sometimes the brothers were a little fearful of the great number, but even until the end Father Maximilian would not give up this form of propaganda.

He gave his readers his absolute confidence, but he engaged their consciences. For instance, he wrote: "We offer free subscriptions very willingly to anyone who is unable to offer anything for the work of the Immaculata, *even by depriving himself a little.*"

The shot hit the mark. As a result, touching letters started to pour in. One read: "I gave up smoking in order to be able to pay my subscription and that of one of my neighbors, who is an infidel." Another: "After High Mass, I had the habit of going to the tavern. I stopped going there and offer these few pennies to the Immaculata." Still another: "Instead of buying myself a dress, I send you the money. This will allow you to offer a few free subscriptions." With his unfailing instinct, Father Maximilian had chosen the right plan. There are among our people fathomless resources of generosity, but to make them vibrate we must first extend confidence.

The workingman and the peasant recognized himself in these brothers, sons of the soil who were working so hard for the glory of the Immaculata. Father Maximilian had struck upon the excellent idea of publishing reports with photographs of the brothers in religious garb putting the review to press. This was truly revolutionary. Until then, most people naïvely thought that a religious did nothing but pray all day and had nothing in common with the workingman. As a result, many candidates applied, but on the condition that they be able to work with Father Maximilian. The situation was becoming delicate and the long-established conventual customs and routines were straining like old barrels with new wine. Father Maximilian was in process of discovering an unprecedented formula of religious life admirably adapted to the needs of the apostolate in the world of today: *Worker Brothers in a workingman's world.*

Fortunately, the superiors did not see the future, for, had they done so, they would have been alarmed. The grain of mustard was growing slowly but vigorously and was becoming a fact to be reckoned with. "Have we the right to reject candidates because they place the condition of working with this nut(!) Father Maximilian?" they asked themselves with dismay. For, truly these superiors were good religious, and to impede a genuine vocation was to them sinful. If only this intrepid priest would give them peace! If only he would take responsibility! But no, instead he writes: "I will blindly fulfill all your desires, because they express to me the will of the Immaculata." What a plague he is! Contradicting him would be easy enough, but who would dare to hinder the plans of the Immaculata?

"Then," they mused, "let him alone for the present; we will see later . . . " But "later" will be too late for restraint. The City of the Immaculata with its seven hundred brothers could not be dissolved in an instant. A review reaching for a circulation of one million does not obey like a door-tending brother. The good Fathers, and especially those who did not believe in him, were one day to find themselves completely overwhelmed by the work of this "dreamer" who competed with the latest industrial enterprises and was aflame with love. The perfect workman, the specialist in a Franciscan habit, living his consecration to the full—what is more marvelous and more unprecedented? And what is more real, more *actual?*

Vestiges of the feudal system in Poland had dug a wide separation between priests and "lay" brothers. The latter, representing an inferior class, were engaged in hard toil and lived apart. At the foundation of the Order, however, such had not been the intention of Saint Francis, himself a simple brother. In returning to the original idea, Father Maximilian was on the way to revealing the extraordinary opportunities of the work and thought of the Poverello. The removal of class distinction was a fundamental need. The advancement of the working class was a current fact, and it was urgently necessary to give it the proper direction. For *progress either is spiritual or it is not progress at all.*

Father Maximilian never found fault with progress. He kept pace with the times as have few of his contemporaries. And he knew that his laboring brothers, consecrated by the total gift of self to the cause of the Immaculata as true laborers and ardent apostles, would one day have an immense mission to accomplish in a world of labor. The world of the workingman, now in the embryonic stage, is the bone of contention between two religions, two *mystiques,* which struggle without mercy—that of the Christ of Catholicism and that of the new Prometheus of Communism. Perhaps the army of the Immaculata which Father Maximilian continues to recruit from his place in heaven will one day have a decisive word to say in this struggle. *Cunctas haereses SOLA interemisti.** Has not Mary succeeded in destroying all heresies?

He was indeed an incomparable educator. His genius caused a creaking in the framework of a conventual life that had become perhaps a bit too set. Lay brothers, who had consecrated themselves whole and entire to the service of the Immaculata, were promoted to the foreground, which until then had been reserved for the priests. In his emphasis on the religious brotherhood Father Maximilian was simply going back to the primitive ideal and was obeying the express wish of the founder, whose democratic ideas had brought about a revolution in his day. He approached the Poverello, how-

---

*"You ALONE have crushed all heresies."

ever, in more than one trait: his ardent love for holy poverty; his heroic obedience and his desire for marytrdom; above all, his measureless and overflowing charity. It was through this love that he won all hearts. How he loved his "little children," the brothers! We have several photographs showing him with groups; they listen, literally drinking in his words, and press close to him as little chicks around the mother hen.

He had an exquisite tenderness with souls. Always extravagant in love, he took time daily to write letters six pages long to one scrupulous person. Friars could always knock on his door, whatever the hour of night. With what love he welcomed "his little lost sheep, his prodigal sons"! Is it surprising that vocations were numerous? Moreover, he did not admit to the service of the Immaculata all applicants merely for the sake of manpower. He took only the carefully selected and did not hesitate to send away specialized technicians when he discovered that their intentions were not sufficiently pure. With Father Maximilian it was all or nothing; and he would not tolerate halfway measures.

* * *

Meanwhile, at Grodno, the good old Fathers were murmuring among themselves. "Has anyone ever seen simple Brothers given such important charges and put on equal footing with the clerical members of the community, assuming the same responsibilities? Why, he turns the world upside down! Come, let us keep each in his proper place! Besides, what will he do with this overflow of vocations? Prudence demands a certain proportion between priests and Brothers. It is very well to admit them, but if bankruptcy should come, Father Maximilian . . . ! What will we do with them when they are old and decrepit? Would it not be better to hire simple workmen?" And so run the verbatim testimonies.

To all these objections Father Maximilian had only one answer: to be able to work for the Immaculata, *one must be consecrated*. He would have preferred to discontinue the review rather than place it in indifferent hands. The modern apostolate requires modern apparatus, indeed, but only under such conditions as would safeguard the primacy of the spiritual. The work of the Immaculata would not be a perfect enterprise if it were *simply* commercial, even if it met with modern technical requirements and was flawlessly written. The work of the Immaculata is infinitely MORE than that!

In short, what he was about to effect poorly, simply, humbly—or, better yet, what his Lady and his Patroness (in the strong sense of the term) condescended to accomplish through his docile mediacy—was the consecration of the working world of today and tomorrow and *the spiritual uplift of the workingman.*

Like a battalion, humanity progresses with a vanguard to lead the serried masses. These leaders are the spiritual summits that determine the climate of the plains. Such is the admirable reason of the religious Orders: the Lord invites them to the tremendous responsibility of being the summits. Through the ages, each social form calls for its consecration and its spiritual vanguard. There was a time when the forms of chivalry, half-barbarian and half-pagan, were confronted with the ideal of the chivalry of Christ, the defender of the persecuted and the innocent. But the epoch in which we live opens other tournaments to man intoxicated by his technical conquests. The modern chivalry is the world of the working-class progressing with its vast potentialities and its immense deficiencies. Is it sufficient to give it back to Christ the way it is? Does it not need as model and springboard a renewed religious Order of workers, genuine but consecrated workers living their lives of labor fully and ever revitalizing them by a complete and unreserved self-surrender? This is one way to transform the machine into a canticle of praise.

Through the Incarnation, Almighty God yielded Himself to time. As a corollary, the most heavenly works obey the laws of growth. The work of Father Maximilian fits into this pattern, for at Grodno he groped along and only in the translucence of his guide, the Immaculata, did he discover by slow degrees the reason for his work.

The brothers worked in perfect joy, although they were in need of the very necessities of life. From time to time, Father Maximilian went to Warsaw and brought back "gifts" for them—not really gifts, for these were not expected, but tools and supplies for the work.

"We would run like children to meet him and happily take the things he brought back to us: for Friar Albert, a few pounds of printers' type and a box of colored ink; for Friar Joachim, several thimbles and some brass wire; for the administration offices, a few reams of paper."

For nothing in the world would Father Maximilian have hired a cab. Though the station was four miles from the friary, he carried his "gifts" on his back. While returning one winter day, he slipped on the ice and fell beneath the weight of his burden. He concluded his account of the mishap with the gleeful remark, "You see, my Brothers, I fell so gracefully that not one box is broken!"

This little group of Franciscans was so poor that boots (which are indispensable in Poland) and overcoats were shared in common, since each religious could not be equipped with a complete wardrobe. On days off they had to search out what they needed. Brother Albert used Father Melchior's blouse. Brother Gabriel would fumble through the meager wardrobe of Brother Pascal and wear his coat more often than the owner would. Fortunately, Father Maximilian wore the same size shoe as Brother Zeno, who always wore them and "gave" them back to Father Maximilian only when the priest was going to Warsaw. Only Father Maximilian's old coat did not change hands, for the simple reason that he had to use it at night in place of a blanket.

In 1925, the year of Jubilee, the workers of Our Lady at Grodno decided upon a new effort that seemed more or less pure folly: namely, the publication of a special calendar of sixty pages singing the praises of the Immaculata. To achieve the prodigious goal of 1200 copies it would be necessary to work for three months without taking any recreation, to sacrifice more sleep, and to work like madmen. In the "editorial room," Father Maximilian had scarcely finished the article he was writing when the typographer would come "to snatch it from his hands" and pass it on to the composing room. Then the priest-editor would change his profession, put on his printer's frock and either turn the famous wheel or press the pedal of the poor, stubborn old machine.

At night he would send the young brothers to the dormitory and stay alone with Brother Albert to round off the work of the day. Sometimes this would take hours. One night, Father Maximilian was on the way to dictate corrections with an oil lamp in his hand; suddenly it fell with a crash and startled him out of sleep. Another time, he appeared in the morning with a large bump on his forehead and laughingly explained to the anxious friars that on the evening before he had fallen asleep while reciting his breviary.

The famous calendar certainly did not follow the rules of advertising. At the very beginning the editor pointed out all its defects and apologized for them. Furthermore, no price was set and the editor simply declared: "Dear readers, if you believe that this calendar can kindle hearts with even one spark of love for the Immaculata, kindly spread it around you . . . "

The calendar proved to be an investment and brought in a sum of money truly unexpected. One can say that the year of Jubilee marked a stage in the development of the work. The chronicles of Niepokalanow talk about a real "shower of roses." It was exactly that. Father Maximilian had prayed for years for the canonization of the little Carmelite who had just been elevated to the altars in glory. The charming wonder-worker is well-versed in gratitude: in 1925, the number of brothers and the circulation were doubled!

This ever-swelling project caused further creaking at the seams of the conventual framework, and the older priests of the friary were dismayed. The Provincial opportunely arrived for a visit. He ascertained the astonishing progress of the review, blessed it, asked to be admitted to the Militia of the Immaculata, and directed the Guardian of the friary, Father Fordon, who was already won over to the work, to provide a wing of the house for the printing establishment.

After his departure, the opposition raised its head. It was prepared to sabotage these plans. The brothers were disheartened. What could they do? One of them had an ingenious idea: since they had permission and were thus equipped with holy obedience, they would hasten events and face the opposing friars with the accomplished fact.

No sooner said than done. They got up like thieves in the night and went quietly to the old dining room that had just been given them. Armed with picks and axes, they began to tear down the useless partitions and demolish the ovens. The convent was so vast and the priests were sleeping so peacefully that the din and clangor awakened no one. When the brother cook came as usual at six o'clock to prepare breakfast, he nearly fell over "at the sight of these fanatics, black as demons, who were sending up great clouds of soot and dust."

To their questioners the brothers candidly explained that they wanted to gain time and that, since they had the necessary authorization, it seemed better not to delay in taking possession of the premises.

This act won for them the stern condemnation of the older priests. "They call us crazy and say we ought to be put into strait jackets," calmly writes the brother chronicler, "but we put up with it in a spirit of penance and humility."

One would expect Father Maximilian to quiet down after this exploit. But no, the huge dining room, finally reconstructed for printing, needed equipment. No one knew where he obtained the money for these extensive purchases. The fact is that on a certain day immense and mysterious crates appeared at the station of Grodno. The machines caused a sensation. The brothers had never experienced such a sight—so perfect and at the same time so complicated. They did not know where to begin. There were dramatic moments when certain motors, put in motion, could not be stopped, and one of them "began to explode like a machine gun," stirring up a real panic among the brothers. Even Father Maximilian, usually so resourceful, could not make it out. The machines were there, but how to subdue them?

It chanced at that precise moment that a mechanic, a specialist in that line, applied for admission "to the crew of the Immaculata." Under the expert hands of this Brother Francis de Sales, the most reluctant machines became like lambs and everything was getting on prosperously.

The purchase of the diesel motor was like a real poem. Father Maximilian and Brother Zeno went to the house of Mr. Borowski, the owner. On the way he recited his habitual endless chain of Hail Mary's. When they arrived at the place, they saw above the motor a little image of the Blessed Virgin.

"This motor belongs to us," whispered Father Maximilian, "watch!"

And, in fact, at the end of a rather long conversation the sale was concluded with a reduction of thirty-five per cent. Mr. Borowski himself installed the motor in the new printing establishment. During the installation he secretly confided to one of the friars that he had not been to confession in twenty years. This brother repeated it to another—under the seal of secrecy, of course—and soon the sad news went the rounds of the community. What to do? Mr. Borowski did not even want to hear the word *confession*.

"Pray, my sons," Father Maximilian said. "Prayer can do everything."

One evening, the brothers invited their "dear impenitent" to go to church with them.

"But I never set foot inside a church," he protested in bewilderment.

"That does not matter," replied a friar. "One has to start some day! No one will see you, because you will be with us in the choir stalls behind the altar."

That seemed to settle it, for he went along. Unfortunately, or by design, he had to kneel awkwardly on a priedieu to which was attached a screen. Father Maximilian passing by saw the trap. Rejoicing, he put on his confessional stole, sat down behind the screen, and asked: "Well, my son, how long since your last confession?"

"Our friend, Mr. Borowski, was cornered," related the chroniclers. "After a long time, he arose with tearstained face, confessed and absolved. . . . After that, time spent in church never seemed long to him."

"You see, my Brothers, how the Blessed Virgin has rewarded his services to her?" beamed the priest.

*   *   *

One would have supposed that the workers of Our Lady would now enjoy a certain period of calm in the plan of work finally adopted. It was not so. The methods of the Immaculata are quite different. Progress is made, but through the Cross and in proportion to the trials. As it happened, the year 1926 saw a hailstorm burst upon the enterprise at Grodno.

There is no kind
of heroism a soul
cannot achieve
with the help of
the Immaculata.

—*Blessed Maximilian*

Blessed Maximilian Kolbe as a young boy. It was during this period of his life that the great Marian apostle had a prophetic vision of what great things God had planned for him. The Blessed Virgin appeared to him and offered him two crowns — one white (for purity) the other red (representing martyrdom). Young Raymond Kolbe stretched out his hands for both.

Poland's "Black Madonna," enshrined in the Pauline Fathers' monastery at Czestochowa (below), has been the rallying point of Polish patriotism for the last 500 years, especially in times of suppression and persecution. Blessed Maximilian added to the Marian heritage of the Poles a world-wide devotion to Mary in her Immaculate Conception.

Maria Dabrowska, who as a young girl wanted to enter the convent, married the tall, blond, very gentle, and religious Jules Kolbe. The mother of Bl. Maximilian Kolbe was an energetic, pious, industrious woman who ruled her home masterfully and quite firmly.

Below: The Seraphic College where Blessed Maximilian studied for the priesthood. While a student here he founded the Militia of Mary Immaculate on October 17, 1917.

Bl. Maximilian as a student in Rome, where he founded the Militia of Mary Immaculate to combat the forces of evil and bring about a revitalization of the apostolate through the most effective material means (the best and most modern inventions were to be used in the apostolate) and the most fruitful spiritual way — total consecration to Mary Immaculate — to be instruments in her hands for the conquest of as many souls as possible.

Below: The national center of the Militia in Italy which is situated in the Tre Fontane district of Rome. The church was dedicated in 1965.

Grodno, Poland, where Blessed Maximilian expanded so rapidly he had to find larger quarters for his printing enterprise.

Blessed Maximilian (center, with hands on his knees) with a group of his first Brothers at Grodno. His blood-brother, Father Alphonse, is at his left.

The first "inhabitant" at the "City of the Immaculata" was Mary herself; her statue was set up in a vacant field.

Above: Buildings were continually being constructed to meet the need of an ever expanding apostolate, and to house the many young men who wished to follow in Bl. Maximilian's footsteps.

A lumber mill was built and operated by Brothers to speed up the construction of buildings and keep costs down.

The photoengraving department at the "City of the Immaculata."

Large rotary presses ran day and night to produce the many publications printed at the "City." Among the magazines, the largest in circulation was the "Knight of the Immaculata"; a million copies were printed in December 1938.

Right: A battery of Linotype machines at the "City." These Brothers, who were totally dedicated to God's service, quickly achieved the professional level. Of the thirty Brother-Linotypists, four had the highest rating in Poland in setting type.

A profession ceremony at the "City of the Immaculata." Personal sanctification, through the three religious vows of poverty, chastity and obedience, was the yardstick of true progress at the "City."

Fr. Maximilian stopped over in Rome on his way to the foreign missions to eventually establish a "City" in Japan. He visited the coliseum, where he no doubt thought of the "red crown of martyrdom" which the Immaculata offered him as a child. The Friar on his left is Bro. Zeno, who is still a missionary in Japan. His great charity work among the poor and disaster victims, has earned him one of Japan's highest awards and the title, "Father of the Poor."

The greater portion of the community of over 750 Franciscan religious (mostly Brothers) who joined Blessed Maximilian in spreading devotion to Mary Immaculate.

Typesetters in Japan during the early days of the "Garden of the Immaculata."

Father Maximilian was a real father to all his Brothers, not only inspiring their confidence, but by his example made personal holiness seem quite easy.

> "The more powerful and courageous a soul becomes with the help of God's grace, the greater the cross God places on its shoulders, so that it might mirror as closely as possible the image of the Crucified in its own life."
>
> —Bl. Maximilian Kolbe

Left: Entrance to the infamous concentration camp of Auschwitz. The cynical words above the entrance read: "Work brings freedom." Middle picture: The cell block where Father Maximilian was confined at Auschwitz. Bottom picture shows the Brothers from the "City of the Immaculata" being marched away to a concentration camp. Right: 1941 Prisoner 16670, now known as Blessed Maximilian Kolbe.

Left: Ex-Sergeant, Francis Gajowniczek, the man whose life was saved by Father Maximilian Kolbe. The two paintings below depict the sadistic beating which a cruel camp trustee inflicted on Fr. Maximilian and the heroic offering Fr. Maximilian made of his life to spare that of the young Polish soldier. Sentenced to a death by slow, agonizing starvation, he was murdered by an injection of carbolic acid to make room for more victims in the starvation cell bunker.

"Father Maximilian is a kind of an individual that the world cannot easily dismiss him. His life is one that cannot be filed away in archives. . . . Even in the framework of religious life he must have risen above the established order of things and maybe his religious contemporaries also wanted to place him in a line, but Father Maximilian said: 'I form a new line.' And he placed the Franciscan religious family in that line. And this was good because this was a particularly great grace in those times for the Franciscan religious family. And therefore this person, who towers above us all, will not permit himself, as they say, to be easily classified. He will always and for a long time tower above all of us by a head. . . . "

—Cardinal Wyszynski, Primate of Poland

Top picture: Cardinal Wyszynski delivers a homily on the heroic virtues of Blessed Maximilian Kolbe in the room of the Seraphic College in Rome where the Blessed lived as a student for the priesthood. Above: A session of priests and prelates studying the life and works of Fr. Maximilian in preparation for his beatification.

The press apostolate of the Brothers in the "City of the Immaculata" in Poland has been suppressed, but they have directed their energies towards other things, among which was the building and furnishing of a huge basilica as a beautiful testimony to the tremendous love which Fr. Maximilian and they themselves have for Our Lady.

Father Maximilian had a serious relapse. His superiors sent him at once to Zakopane, where he stayed for six months. His brother, Father Alphonse Kolbe, replaced him and asked only one thing: to follow him step by step. Unfortunately, he had neither Father Maximilian's stature nor his genius. However, his humility supplied what he lacked in talent, and he was always to be Father Maximilian's most faithful collaborator. For the present he had to solve all problems alone, since his brother had received orders not even to think about the publication. Naturally, he gave the order his heroic and literal obedience. The next setback was the death of the veteran of the crew; Brother Albert Olszakowski went to swell the ranks of "the troops in heaven."

Amidst these reverses, which could hinder or even stop its growth, the little blue review expanded more and more, sending up its circulation like tendrils, despite all human predictions.

At Zakopane, Father Maximilian again took up his role of the sick man. He suffered and prayed. He spent his whole day in prayer.

"When at times I am tempted to worry," he wrote to his brother, "I immediately say to myself: 'Silly one, why do you worry? Is this *your* work? If all belongs to the Immaculata, will she not attend to it? Then let her lead you!' "

10

The Master Painter
and Her Broom

THE FOUNDING OF NIEPOKALANOW

Above all, we should not look upon Father Maximilian as a sort of superman disdainfully beyond the reach of ordinary human suffering. Saints suffer as we do, even more than we, for they are gifted with such keen sensibilities that a mere trifle can affect them. The essence of suffering is its apparent absurdity, its element of "What is the use?" Like death, which it anticipates, it is a negation of the integrity of nature. The Cross will not cease to be a "scandal" until the end of time.

The saints do not escape suffering, do not dominate it; they simply embrace it in full darkness, in the paradoxical ignorance of faith. The seed that dies knows nothing of the future harvests; otherwise, where would be the cost? The grain that dies remains buried in the earth. It is the sun that brings it forth, but the grain knows nothing of this. Then come the day when it makes its dazzling discovery.

Father Maximilian's second retirement to Zakopane was the greatest ordeal of his life. Like a disabled soldier evacuated from the front, he felt utterly useless. The doctors did not give him much hope. In his letters he often alluded to his death: "For the sake of the work, it would perhaps be better that I do not return."

His physical suffering was tinged with the agonizing thought that he was a burden or perhaps even a hindrance. He was in the dark, saw nothing, understood nothing; he lived deep within himself. A commonplace trial, but how full of anguish! In his letters to his brother, he steeled himself against revealing too much. He formerly wrote from the abundance of his heart, in the full joy of light; but now he limited himself to strictly technical problems, to the answering of questions. Of his soul he said nothing; to his ideal he made but infrequent and timid allusion. This was not the time for words, but for fruitful silence. His Lady and Mistress made him pass through a novitiate more trying than the one of Lwow, and later he would often speak of this period as "the ordeal by fire." By the law of sanctity, a soul of his temper must pass through the phase of abandonment.

In a revealing letter, he put the novices of Grodno on guard against attachment to sensible graces. "You must expect periods of darkness, anxiety, uncertainty, fears, temptations, sometimes harassing physical suffering; but also mental suffering, which is infinitely more acute. . . . "

In this violent tempest, what was his buoy, his lighthouse, his only hope? She who has always conquered evil and who is bathed at every instant in pure light. If he no longer saw her, so much the better. Is it not the proof of deepest love to give wtihout asking anything in return? Henceforth, in his letters and in all his writings there was a new note of poignant sweetness expressing a charter of complete surrender. The pact was consummated in the dark night of the soul.

"Have no confidence in yourselves, but in all your temptations and trials surrender to the Immaculata and surely you will triumph." And he finished the same letter with this touching desire: "I want you to love her so much that you will be completely unable to live without her."

*   *   *

Indeed, it was no human remedy that restored this man who had been so close to death. Naturally reserved, Father Maximilian later made this single discreet allusion: "When all means proved to be powerless, when I was given up for lost and my superiors found me unfit for any work, then the Immaculata came to gather up this poor wreck who was good only for the waste basket. She took this good-for-nothing and used him to spread the glory of God! Let us imagine a great painter who would paint a masterpiece with a shabby broom. Our Lady is the painter, and the broom is myself."

The period of preparation had lasted long enough. Henceforth, no success, no conquest nor victory could tempt him to pride, for he was only a poor, useless old broom—but in the hand of a great artist!

Meanwhile, in spite of all predictions, the publication at Grodno prospered, and the circulation continued to dart upward: in 1924, 12,000 copies; in 1925, 30,000; in 1926, 45,000. The ancient friary of Grodno was filled to overflowing. The older Fathers murmured, but let us not be too quick to blame them. Life in the company of the saints is not always comfortable. True, Father Maximilian was not there; but his brother, Father Alphonse, a real "lamb of the Good Lord" like Brother Leo of the *Fioretti,* had only one ambition: namely, to imitate his brother in everything. This meant, "Go ahead, always ahead!"

The unsympathetic priests were practical. The ideal of the Poverello had shrivelled a bit in the course of the centuries; we are no longer in the heroic period of the Order. The older Fathers did not approve of these venturesome risks. Their practical minds dictated that they set limits to the project and bank the capital, which would comfortably finance the enterprise and provide income for the friary's expenses.

They could not understand what seemed to them foolhardy mass production. Once more, we should be indulgent toward them. Saints are canonized only after death; but during their lifetime we help the Good Lord make them saints by our opposition. Surely, nothing roots them more firmly in perfect charity than persecution by the good, by their brothers. The Lord has even made it clear to us that in persecuting them we will actually think that we bring glory to God! These persecutions, then, are quite normal.

Divine Providence intended the laborers of the Madonna to work elsewhere. It was necessary then to oust them from Grodno, where they had begun to feel themselves more and more crowded, not only in soul but in body as well. This was one of those crises of growth usually found in the work of the Lord.

In the matter of saving the profits Father Maximilian held firm. The work of the Immaculata should not be a lucrative enterprise! "Our purpose," he wrote from Zakopane, "is to conquer for Christ, to win all the world and all souls without exception for the Immaculata—never material gain, as a little while ago one of our Fathers thought. To act on his advice and curtail the work and the purchase of machines in order to have an income would be to mistake the means for the end. 'We will have a friary income'—but meanwhile, souls are being lost, Satan multiplies his conquests, and the atheistic press prospers. Mediocrity! Nothing more!"

Although generally calm, he could bear it no longer, for he was touched to the quick. Rarely since the Poverello have the rights and privileges of holy poverty been defended with a more tenacious ardor. It is not the letter that he defends, but the spirit. His poverty has a very modern aspect. It can be summed up in two phrases: nothing for us; all for God and the Immaculata. For us, the worst everything: plain food, miserable huts, patched clothing. For her, model workshops, the latest improvements in machinery, all the products of modern technique, the fastest means of transportation.

He would have liked to offer to the Lady of his heart all the first fruits of human genius; breathe into the most technical work a soul and an ardent ideal; sanctify the workshop, the machine, all work, both menial and highly specialized. He would incorporate even the tools into the canticle of praise.

Evidently, these ideas must have bewildered those of the friars who were literal-minded. However, they were not the only ones to be scandalized. One day, a certain prelate came to look around and, as he pointed to one of the powerful machines, he said to Father Maximilian, "What would Saint Francis do if he could see these expensive machines?"

"He would tuck up his sleeves, your Excellency, and begin to work with us."

Let us note now that heroism is contagious and that certain confreres who had been most strenuous objectors became with time his ardent collaborators. One does not frequent the company of the saints with immunity.

*   *   *

Father Maximilian came back from Zakopane when conditions at Grodno were critical. It was imperative that this busy colony of friars swarm to another location, and as soon as possible. But where? How?

If heretofore in our story we have more than once brushed against marvels of the supernatural, from now on we will be obliged to accustom ourselves to an atmosphere of the miraculous. Father Maximilian, who returned not cured but stimulated by "the ordeal by fire," was definitely master of his means—that is to say, fully "liberated." The Madonna could proceed.

"Coincidences" increased and "Chance" was making sport. News came in the summer of 1927 that very near Warsaw there was land for sale. Father Maximilian entered into negotiations, went to see it, became enthusiastic, and on August 6, in the middle of the field set up a statue of the Blessed Virgin, saying to her in a low voice: "Immaculata, deign to take into your possession this field and this land, for it is exactly what we want."

However, the Provincial found the conditions too onerous and refused permission. Father Maximilian submitted as usual without a word of discussion. He had only one fear; it was "to interfere with the will of the Immaculata as manifested in the will of his superiors by forcing his will on them." With heavy heart he went to inform the owner, Prince Drucki-Lubecki, that the purchase would not take place.

"What shall I do with the statue?" asked the Prince.

"Let it remain where it is," was the reply.

The Prince thought for a moment, then abruptly decided. "Well, take the land with it! I give it to you for nothing."

Then and there Father Maximilian wrote a letter to the Provincial to announce "the new state of affairs."

The final permission arrived at Grodno. Father Maximilian opened the letter in the workshop, where they were printing the latest issue of the review. Then he called to the brother laborers: "Let us fall on our knees, my sons, to say thank you to the Blessed Virgin."

And they recited three Hail Mary's in the midst of the whirring of the motors.

The first group of workers left immediately to prepare for installation. Under the smiling eyes of the Immaculata, they began to build rough barracks. They were too poor to treat themselves to the luxury of hired labor and they had to economize strictly in time, labor and money in order not to curtail the publishing of the review. The peasants of the surrounding country, filled with pity, brought provisions to these religious, who were "not at all proud," who scarcely thought of food but came to their work in the morning with only a large loaf of bread. In addition to bringing food, the peasants also lent a helping hand. A sacred alliance was concluded in the sharing of the same sweat and the same work. Henceforth, people would call the city of the Virgin "our" Niepokalanow.

Father Maximilian was the first at work and did not spare himself. It was the month of October, and every morning the surrounding fields were white with frost. He often had to sleep in the open air or in the barracks with its gaping holes for windows. He went to Warsaw every day and came back loaded with packages. Only a year previous, the doctors had prescribed for him "a very calm and regular life, most nourishing food, much rest and sleep, and above all no carrying of heavy loads." How did he manage? That is the secret of her who is the "Health of the Sick!" Neither in the year of foundation nor in the following years did he suffer grave relapse, in spite of overtiring work, very little sleep, and often unhealthy climate. He was to stay with his task until death.

The Madonna's workmen left Grodno on November 21, 1927, the feast of the Presentation. They arrived at Niepokalanow the next day and had to help immediately with the building of sheds needed for the printing establishment. They cooked in the open air, and not too bountifully, for there was no time to lose. Fortunately, the peasants of that area, stirred by so much enthusiasm and such poverty, attended to the feeding of these young workingmen in religious garb and called them simply "little brothers." There were 20 friars at the time—two priests and 18 religious Brothers.

In the beginning, the privations were extreme and they had to beg for the necessities of life . . . "All for the Immaculata!" But the faithful Virgin watched over the progress entrusted to her care. "Even our Jewish neighbors were helping us," marvels Brother Zeno, the "Brother Juniper" of this Franciscan community.

Obviously, new vocations had to stand up under rigid test. "When I arrived," a brother told me, "I received a real shock. I asked a farmer, 'Where is the friary?'

" 'There,' he answered.

" 'I don't see a friary there.'

" 'Look again,' he said. 'Do you see those sheds?'

"I saw only some low wooden huts covered with a rough coat of whitewash.

" 'Is that the friary?' I asked in surprise.

" 'It certainly is! Inside they seem very content. Always singing.'

"It was Father Maximilian himself who welcomed me," continues this brother. "He was coming from work and seemed very tired. He looked at me with his eyes which were as kind as a mother's, and said, 'You must be very tired and hungry. Come, my son.'

"He gave me something to eat and something to drink. Then he said, 'If you love the Blessed Virgin, if you belong entirely to her, you will be happy, my son—so happy!' He smiled as he spoke and seemed radiantly happy.

"I thought to myself, 'What he says, he himself lives.' And suddenly I felt very happy myself and have been happy ever since. I found in him both a father and a mother."

His affection is a trait that the testimonies of the brothers indicate with a touching insistence.

"I do not think," one of them writes, "that parents have ever loved their own children so much—so providently and so tenderly—as Father Maximilian has loved us." And another: "I have loved him as much as my own father and mother and even more, for really I have found in him both father and mother." And yet another: "I felt myself as near to him as a little child on the heart of his mother."

Father Maximilian had a very clear understanding of this spiritual paternity. With Saint Paul, he often repeated in his admirable letters: "In Jesus Christ I hold you as most dear children." He often recommended that their superiors treat them "maternally, for in order to come here they have abandoned all, and sometimes at great sacrifice. They must, then, find in us a new family, a real one."

11

Life in the City of The Immaculata

Since the day they found themselves "at home" or, to be more exact, in the domain of the Immaculata—for that is the meaning of "Niepokalanow"—their joyous daring was unlimited. There was a constant ascent to the summits of pure heroism. "There is no time to lose!" they said. "Our objective, to use a military term so dear to our founder, is the ENTIRE WORLD. Then, forward from conquest to conquest!"

It was a spiraling flight, which dazzled some and disconcerted others, turning loose enthusiasms and a real tempest of hatred and persecution. The circulation of the review increased each year in almost geometrical proportions: in 1927, 50,000 copies; in 1928, 81,000; in 1929, 117,500; in 1930, 292,750; in 1931, 432,000; in 935, 700,000; and in 1939, 1,000,000.

At this stage there was only the monthly review. But why stop there? Were there not the children? A new publication, *The Little Knight of the Immaculata,* was begun for them. Furthermore, the Polish language is not read outside Poland. "We need a world press agency," said Father Maximilian. He therefore launched the Latin publication *Miles Immaculatae (Soldier of the Immaculata),* intended to rally the clergy of all races and all languages.

Nor were these all. For a long time the bishops of Poland had been calling for a newspaper under militant Catholic management. It was to be well written but suited to the needs of the people; it was imperative that it be above and beyond all party differences and petty interests. More than one attempt had been made, but after a few months it was always the same sad outcome—bankruptcy. It was next to impossible to maintain a newspaper on a frankly Catholic basis, in an atmosphere of truth. Moreover, the great press of Poland was on guard against competitors.

What so many others had tried in vain, Our Lady's task force undertook with immediate success. In May, 1935, the first number of the *Maly Dziennik* (*Little Journal*) appeared, winning a vast reading public at once. Very well written, inexpensive, printed in blue and white, the colors of the Immaculata, it penetrated everywhere and was sold everywhere by eager newspaper boys, delighted to be enlisted "in the service of Our Lady."

The circulation was so rapid and so extensive that the directors of the massive secular press were struck with consternation. They certainly had not foreseen such competition from those "poor brothers." It was infuriating to watch the figures of their business melt away while this "leaf of cabbage," as they contemptuously called the *Little Journal,* spread everywhere, going straight to the heart of the people.

"You hold the trump card," was their enraged complaint, "since labor costs you nothing!"

"Well, after all, why do you not try the same system?" was Father Maximilian's smiling retort.

The ridiculously low price of a few pennies was not the only secret of the paper's marvelous success: What the directors of the big newspapers did not know and would never understand was the true starting point of the *Little Journal.* For nine days before the appearance of the first issue, the three hundred and twenty-seven Franciscan men of labor prayed night and day before the Blessed Sacrament. They fasted and did penance, fervently recommending their noble project to the "Patroness of the enterprise." Then and only then did they put their powerful presses in motion. With these highly trained workmen, prayer *always* preceded action. The hierarchy of values was jealously observed.

Although the spiritual was given first place, the material side did not suffer in the least. Quite the contrary. These contemplatives were outstanding technicians, qualified in many fields and always alert to improvement and progress. The practical genius of Father Maximilian sought holy workmen at Niepokalanow, veritable saints formed by perfect fidelity to duty. One cannot run machines with a Hail Mary, but one can convert the flawless rumbling of a rotary press into a Magnificat! The good priest would not tolerate half-hearted amateurs and he often repeated in his letters the old adage: *Age quod agis*—that is, "Attend to the business you have at hand."

To understand this more clearly, let us visit the friars on the premises of Niepokalanow. We pass over the interval of nine years that has elapsed since the day when Father Maximilian came to enthrone the statue of the Immaculata in this desert.

We are faced by an entire village, which, from a distance, looks like an industrial town. The friar attending the door smiles and leads us to the Guardian, the director of this vast enterprise. We enter a small, whitewashed room of about nine square yards. The only furniture is a table, two stools, two shelves lined with books and, in a corner, an iron bed and a wash basin. The furniture is white wood. On the table, there is a telephone and, of course, a statuette of the Immaculata. This strict poverty that we meet everywhere emits a character of nobility all its own. At Niepokalanow nothing is common.

The Guardian seems very young and has very soft but penetrating eyes. I do not wonder at all that certain friars attribute to him the gift of reading hearts. He wears a bushy graying beard, which he strokes with a certain tranquility, and often smiles with a childlike candor, showing all his teeth. He does not appear sick, but he does seem very much worn out. We learn that he came back from Japan recently.

He welcomes us with Franciscan hospitality and immediately lifts the receiver to inform the brother cook that "there are friends here who look as though they are willing to take a cup of tea." A few moments later, a very young brother radiant with happiness appears, bearing a large tray with a teapot and some tin cups. At Niepokalanow chinaware is banned, and Monsignor the Nuncio and his Eminence the Cardinal must use those same cups—which, moreover, they do with good grace.

The priest answers our questions simply. He very carefully avoids any reference to himself, and we feel that he really considers himself an unimportant figure in this colossal work. Should the question arise, he changes the subject. However, as soon as anyone mentions the Blessed Virgin, he springs to life and, with face aglow, makes some characteristic remark, such as: "She is our whole life. It is she who does everything! Through her, we want to win for Christ every soul in the entire world—those souls that are and those yet to be until the end of time."

He speaks with such a fervent and quivering voice and a face so transfigured that we understand at once what these awkward words are hiding and what resplendent reality has become incarnate in these poor barracks.

We are invited to see the workshops. In each room a statue of the Immaculata is enthroned. Each crew of workers kneels down upon entering, offers a brief prayer before work, and immediately occupies the appointed posts. Silence during work is a strict rule, and they can break it only in cases of real necessity and even then only in a low voice. In the vast halls we hear only the rumbling of the motors, the whistling of the transmissions and the rhythmical noise of the powerful presses that "hand over" each hour 20,000 copies of the review, stitched and ready for shipping. Another crew of workmen immediately takes possession of them for sorting into districts and addressing. To achieve maximum output they work systematically in groups of three which handle the neatly cut stacks.

Dissatisfied with the addressing machines which were imported from abroad, a brother who was a specialist invented a new model, which at once won a prize at the exhibition at Poznan. This machine doubled the previous output. In this shipping department, silence is likewise observed. The young and meditative faces reflect much joy—and a degree of fatigue. It is the end of the day's work. All heads turn toward the Guardian, and all their eyes smile at him. He greets them as usual: "Maria." And they answer softly, pronouncing the same name: "Maria."

Pervading these workshops there is an indefinable atmosphere, an impressive simplicity. The machines, directed by expert and fervent hands, seem really to pray. Strictly technical and performed by highly competent hands, the work is surpassed without fail by an intention of love that transforms it into liturgy. These workers talk of their "Sister Press" and "Brother Motor" in the same accents with which Saint Francis speaks of the birds and flowers. Indeed, he would have known them for his sons by their language.

I suddenly remember how one day Father Maximilian had sung the praise of "Brother Motor" which was about to enter solemnly into service. "What should I wish for it," he said, "except that it faithfully serve its Queen and Mistress? Today it is blessed and it becomes a religious. Then they will start to adjust it; that will be its novitiate. And when they make it run, it will make profession. What more can I wish for it? That it work a long time? That it have a great many companions? That it be efficient? Well, no, I do not wish anything else for it. Whatever it may do, only one thing is of consequence: that it follow blindly the desires of the Blessed Virgin. A good religious, is good, not because he does much, but because he obeys. Thus, 'Brother Motor' will be a good religious if, thanks to the intervention of the brother mechanic, it does what the Immaculata will ask it to do. If she wishes, may it be out of order as soon as tomorrow; if she wishes, may it work a hundred years and more and may it earn what is necessary to procure for us more 'Brother Motors.' "

Is this not the language of the *Fioretti?*

It is surprising that in this "Workers' Republic" there are only six priests but more than seven hundred brothers who have the responsibility of management in the name of holy obedience. In his genius for organization Father Maximilian never wanted blind instruments, and no one desired more than he to train the friars in a sense of responsibility and in the spirit of inventiveness. Each friar has the right to ask to work in the section that suits him best and to apply for a change when he feels himself losing interest. Of course, holy obedience will sometimes keep him where he is, but always for reasons which can be made evident. Father Maximilian detests the absurdity of needless specialization. He desires that each friar know all phases of his specialty and purposely makes him pass from one workshop to another. At Niepokalanow, there are no robots; only workmen proud of their vocations and ennobled by this total gift that transforms them into associates of God.

In the administration offices of Niepokalanow there is a special box with a poster which reads: "Inventions and Projects," where each friar has the right to deposit his ideas for improvement. Under the control of a special committee, these proposals are very often put in force and increase the quality of production. Looking at these open, young and intelligent faces, I am not surprised that Niepokalanow has several patents among its assets.

"Are there many vocations?" we ask the priest.

"Oh, yes, each year about eighteen hundred candidates apply. But we apply rigid screening tests. At the end of these, about a hundred enter, scarcely fifty of whom reach profession. We must be selective because . . . " he hesitates an instant, "Niepokalanow must be a school of saints."

Among the postulants, there are a great many specialized workmen who were successfully earning their living in the world. There are others with college educations: architects, engineers, assistant professors. Niepokalanow is really self-sufficient, for all professions are represented here. It would require an entire chapter, and a most interesting one, to write about their fire department and its wide and numberless achievements.

At first glance, a brother workman cannot be distinguished from the priest-editor. He wears the same kind of religious habit, worn and patched; he eats the same food. Father Maximilian shows no partiality. All priests and brothers are and *must* be treated the same way, and anyone guilty of making an exception to the rule is severely punished. The single privilege of the "chiefs" is to have a private cell with furniture exactly the same as that of the Father Guardian. Most of the brothers sleep in large dormitories.

They tell delightful stories about the righteous anger of Father Maximilian when he discovered that they had secretly granted him some privilege. Every time he found a new garment in his cell, he would invariably ask, "Have all the Fathers as much?" He permitted no exception! Sometimes they had to resort to tricks to make him put on a new sweater or in order to substitute new shoes for his old ones.

Only the sick are privileged. For them there is special cooking, and they receive all the remedies they need, even the most expensive. For them he provides the most qualified specialists, the most expensive cures, the greatest comfort possible. Father Maximilian literally spoils them. He himself has been very sick too long not to know how much one can suffer in an infirmary. Even on the busiest working days he goes on his rounds to visit his "dear sick ones," to tell them how much he needs their help and how all Niepokalanow counts on them. If visitors indiscreetly ask him where in that buzzing hive most work is done, he leads them into the house of rest surrounded by fir trees, answers: "Here," and shows them his "dear sick ones."

In the dining room there are endless tables made of white wood and, naturally, at the end of the room a little altar where the Immaculata presides. The friars pray before meals. How they pray! Each word is carefully measured and carries the mark of an inexpressible fervor. Together in chorus, the friars recite this verse which the visitor at Niepokalanow will hear more than once again: *Deus caritas est, et qui manet in caritate, in Deo manet, et Deus in eo.** In listening to them we feel that we detect their secret. It is love that has united them, it is love that keeps them; not an idea nor a myth, but the One who is Love.

The food is simple, but good and abundant. At Niepokalanow no one is hungry. They all eat from the same kind of tin plates, with the same kind of spoons. On visiting days there is often a *"Deo gratias"* which unties the tongues and

---

*"God is love, and he who abides in love abides in God, and God in him" (1 John 4: 16).

fills the vast dining room with a joyous buzzing. But usually there is a jealously observed silence, for Father Maximilian attaches great importance to it: "How will you hear the voice of God," he says, "if you make too much noise? He speaks to you, but in silence."

The business leaders who come to look around out of simple curiosity—for Niepokalanow begins to have a renown of sanctity as well as of offence—very quickly find themselves astounded and entirely out of place. One of them laughingly said to me one day, "It is very strange, technician and mystic walking arm in arm!"

To really understand these friars, we must follow them to the chapel. It also is a simple shed, pending the future basilica that Father Maximilian will not see. The chapel is filled to capacity with young Franciscans on their knees, praying with such fervent intensity that their faces grow radiant. The rule provides three hours and a half of prayer and meditation each day. But their work is a continuous prayer. Indeed, they have a great many occasions for listening to God—and for hearing Him!

This up-to-date industrial enterprise, which surpasses all records and is considered a model of technical efficiency, has its roots deeply plunged in the supernatural. This is what brings it so much persecution, so much slander, and such angry criticism—not only from the powers of hell but also from the supposedly well-disposed, who like to reconcile God and Mammon!

Nevertheless, even their enemies cannot avoid an occasional compliment. One day, some merchants came to Niepokalanow on business. Having visited everywhere and seen all, one of them made a sort of confession to Father Maximilian.

"I am a Communist." (Before the war, the Communist party had no legal existence in Poland.) "But I must tell you that it is the first time that I have found our ideas realized. You are real Communists!"

He thought it the most beautiful compliment he could invent.

12

World Plan, Part II:
The Far East

There was a time centuries ago when the "Little Brothers" went two by two to announce to the world the good tidings of Christ's gospel. Today, they take advantage of the services of "our Sister Machine" and fling to the four winds innumerable printed pages. Each epoch has its own methods. Father Maximilian joyfully welcomed all discoveries and took possession of them immediately "in order to consecrate them."

"All the fruits of human genius," he used to say, "must be mobilized for the service and glory of God and His Immaculata. On the eve of the war he was in the process of equipping Niepokalanow with an airport with four runways—"for the time being," as he would say. He established a broadcasting station, which was working very well. And he wanted to hire the best actors for Catholic films.

Everything he said and did displayed a joyful, catholic optimism that believed vehemently in the triumph of good. He condemned nothing, he disapproved of nothing—except sin. Far from turning his back upon the age in which he lived, he flung out his arms to embrace it and to hold it. He took care not to call down fire from heaven upon the cockle. The Lord of harvests has from the very beginning sowed wheat; it is useless for the enemy to prowl during the night, for heavy ears of grain dispute the field against the weeds of evil. More than once in his letters we find the appeal for patient winnowing. We must glean from error the grains of truth which are buried in it, he would say, retake what is ours, and leave the rest to die from simple futility.

His method was eminently positive, adaptable and deadly to the adversary, for it took up the enemy's own arms and engaged him on his own ground. It would require an entire chapter to write concerning Father Maximilian and Communism. Had he not the ingenuity to apply the first "Five Year Plan" in the service of the Immaculata at Niepokalanow?

This work and these towering projects should have been enough to satisfy him. But no, his perspective was without horizon. Only one who failed to understand Father Maximilian could think he had forgotten his vow as an ardent young novice, "to conquer the entire world—all souls—for Christ, through the Immaculata." Far from being his sole objective, Poland was only a springboard.

It is here that we must relate the most marvelous episode of this story, one that resembles a fairy tale. Scarcely three years after the foundation of Niepokalanow, when its management would seem to claim full attention and effort, Father Maximilian set out on a mission.

It happened that one day he met some Japanese students on the train. They began to chat and, of course, he offered them miraculous medals, his "shells," which he always carried in his pockets. In exchange, the students gave him some small wooden elephants which they used as charms. After this incident, he frequently gave compassionate thought to these souls who lived without Christ.

After full consideration, he presented himself at the headquarters of his Provincial and, as if it were simply a matters of course, told him that he would like to go to Japan to establish another Niepokalanow.

"Have you the money?" Father Provincial asked in amazement.

"No, Father Provincial."

"Do you know the Japanese language?"

"No."

"Have you at least some friends over there, some support?"

"Not yet, but with the grace of God I will find some."

Let us put ourselves for an instant in the place of the Provincial, the prudent and sensible Father Czupryk. Quite as usual, Father Maximilian begged him above all not to let himself be influenced by him. He told his Provincial that his one desire was to be blindly obedient and that "the Immaculata would manifest her good pleasure to her servant Maximilian through the instrumentality of his superiors." If only he had been disposed to argue! But no, he made only a bland statement of his case: "Here is the plan, foolish though it may seem. And now, Reverend Father, it is for you to decide. You are the spokesman of God. Whatever you may decide, you know very well that I will obey immediately and without comment."

I am sure that after the first bombshell, although Father Maximilian slept like a little child, his superiors passed a sleepless night! How to resist his proposal? Is not Niepokalanow tangible proof that this seven day wonder is always right? He had the gift of making nothingness bear fruit. That which our limited human prudence rates as an adventure in folly may perhaps turn out to be but a normal course in Divine Providence. Suppose, therefore, we give his plan a trial.

Father Maximilian was a wonderfully captivating person. Everyone of good will ended by following him; and the superior who had been the most skeptical grew just as "foolish" and even became his most zealous collaborator. It is in this way that our selfish and cramped hearts expand all at once through contact with a saint. What he tells us we always knew, but somehow we never really understand it. It was a favorite saying of Father Maximilian that *good is more contagious than evil.*

He obtained full authorization at last and on February 26, 1930 set out with four brothers for far distant Japan. He crossed France and stopped at Lourdes and Lisieux; but, as usual, he did not write much about these visits in his letters. We like to imagine him at the Grotto in Lourdes. "You can feel the presence of the Immaculata here," he writes. His letters are impulsive, lively, delightful with a childlike freshness. Obviously to amuse his "little brothers," he wrote: "I have just seen the chessmen that belonged to Saint Thérèse of Lisieux. This is to console our unrepentant chess addicts."

Sometimes in the correspondence of this period the note becomes more serious. "Nothing causes me more suffering than the mediocrity of souls vowed to the Blessed Virgin. I would give my life a thousand times to sanctify them."

"We are the property of the Immaculata, her possession. She has all rights over us. We are her knights, ready to go wherever she bids, willing to do whatever she asks."

"As varied as the flowers of the field are the works within the Church of Christ. Our common end is the cause of the Immaculata."

"Only the fathomless treasures of Providence can compete with the ingots of the Prince of this world. . . . "

"We must sacrifice our life to our ideal, not subordinate our ideal to our life. . . . "

It was a blessed journey that occasioned this precious correspondence. Father Maximilian scarcely speaks of himself, but between the lines his soul shines through. There is always the same full tone, the same rare atmosphere of the summits. Although he sometimes dashes off his scribbled notes, the same overtone of high sanctity vibrates through every line.

They embarked at Marseilles. On the boat and during the landings at port, Father Maximilian made numerous conquests, for his irresistible charm won friends instantaneously. Naturally, as good Franciscans they travelled on the deck and shared the lot of the poorest travellers. Always joyful, obliging and humble, they preached among all these foreigners much more through example than by word. They spent their spare time struggling with the first lessons of the Japanese language.

At Saigon, Father Maximilian had time to come in contact with the clergy of the Annamite rite and obtained on the spot their consent to publish his review. At Shanghai, the Catholic millionaire, Lo Pang Ho, put himself at his service and offered him the money to publish a Chinese review. Unfortunately, the plan failed because other missionaries opposed it.

"The city is divided into spheres of influence," he wrote sadly. "We can act only in the Franciscan zone. The pagans are very willing to help us; all the difficulties come from the Christians."

Leaving two of the Brothers at Shanghai in hopes of starting the M.I. there, Father Maximilian proceeded with the other two to Nagasaki where he landed April 24, 1930. Entering the port, the boat coasted along the picturesque islands, where for three centuries vestiges of Christianity had been preserved. In their bamboo huts they still kept their statues of the Blessed Virgin, "Seibo," sometimes too similar to the one of goddess Kwanom. Under ashes the flame continues to burn. Who will give it back its former brightness? The task of the missionary promised to be arduous, for at great price and as quickly as possible he had to make the blood of the many martyrs bear fruit. Was he thinking of the

Polish Jesuit, Adalbert Mecinski, contemporary of Saint Andrew Bobola, who went to Japan longing to die for the Faith and there won his martyr's palm? Did he reflect upon the innumerable Japanese martyrs, so little known in Europe, who remained intrepid and faithful until the end despite torture and death?

Looking at these islands of the cherry blossoms, Father Maximilian suddenly recalled his beautiful red crown. He asked in a low voice: "Is this, Immaculate Mother, the place that you have prepared for me?"

First of all, the Japanese situation required that the missionary be very clever, very practical and acutely diplomatic. All these qualities the little Polish priest possessed in an eminent degree. He began by carefully observing this strange and unknown world. He very quickly registered all that he wanted to know. Walking the picturesque and swarming streets of Nagasaki, he often lifted his gaze toward the "Hill of Martyrs," where three centuries earlier thousands of Christians had paid with their blood for fidelity to the Faith which the Polish brothers were bringing them from so far away. Could one dream of more powerful allies?

His Excellency, Bishop Hyasaki, of Nagasaki, smiled on hearing the intentions of the missionaries who had recently landed from far-off "Porando." The plan to publish a review without funds seemed to him completely fantastic. But when he learned that Father Maximilian was a doctor of theology and philosophy, he at once asked him to give some courses in his seminary.

Father Maximilian seized the occasion on the wing. "Gladly, your Excellency, but on the condition that you permit us to publish the review."

Disconcerted, the Bishop looked at him. This poor missionary had an air of decision about him. "Let us give the Good Lord a chance," he thought. In his high voice he gave the answer, "It is a bargain; but you must manage for yourself!"

They had arrived on April 24. On May 24, Father Maximilian cabled the following message to Niepokalanow: "Today we are sending out our first issue. Have a printing establishment. Praise be to the Immaculata! Maximilian."

After reading and rereading this telegram, the "little brothers" looked at each other in amazement. Even though they were habitually confident, such success surpassed all their dreams.

What had produced this extraordinary man, who on principle had banned the word *impossible* from his vocabulary? Before all else, he naturally made use of two chief resources: first, prayer; and then a penance which consisted especially in an extreme and perfect poverty. It was this poverty that crushed all suspicion and won at once the hearts of these "dear pagans."

The Japanese are very responsive to the total sacrifice of self to a noble cause. They know how to deprive themselves and they measure the ideal of the stranger by the degree of deprivation that he is capable of imposing upon himself in the name of his ideal. To see these missionaries who were eating poorly, sleeping little, living in the open air, and asking only one thing: namely, to have the Japanese share in the superabundance of joy which was sparkling in their eyes and vibrating in their voices—this made them realize that it was not selfish interest which had brought the Polish missionaries. From the very beginning, Father Maximilian had in them a whole band of willing helpers—even among those who were Protestant. It is interesting to note that the first Japanese translator of the articles which Father Maximilian wrote in Latin or Italian was a Methodist who was soon converted.

As usual, Father Maximilian anticipated great things, expecting contributions from all those of good will, while leaving the rest to the Immaculata.

They began by buying an old printing machine. "It is very much like our granny," writes the missionary. "It is all very rusty and runs only when forced with all our might. Our hands are bloody from forcing it." A little more work was necessary to set up type for the articles translated into Japanese than for Polish articles, and the poor brothers often floundered in the jungle of the two thousand signs of the alphabet. They had great trouble translating the title of the review. Since an exact equivalent of "Immaculata" was non-existent, they had to render it "without sin," that is, *Mugenzai no Seibo no Kishi.*

They lived in a wretched barracks whose roof had holes. "That night we had snow, a real blizzard! It snowed in on our heads, and we had to cover ourselves well for protection. In the morning, our dormitory was all white . . . "

Naturally, they prepared their meals in open air, and it often rained into their large kettle. The native cooking horrified the poor priest and he tried in vain to become accustomed to the Japanese "dainties." One day, while talking about the tribulations that await the missionary, he put at the top of the list—the native cooking!

Father Maximilian was worn out. Violent headaches exhausted him; fever would not leave him. His poor eyes were red from insomnia. A strange infection, caused perhaps by the food which his stomach could not stand, covered him with abscesses so painful that he walked with great misery. During Mass, two brothers had to support him, for he could stand only on one foot. One day, he fell in exhaustion on the road and stayed there unable to move until one of the brothers found him.

However, he held fast and went on working. Far from defeating him, trials spurred him onward. To really understand his indomitable energy, we must go back to its source and call upon the science of saints!

A letter dating from this period sketches the project of other "invasions." "As soon as our work is well established in Japan, I will leave to make foundations in India and afterward at Beirout for the Arabs. I expect to publish the review in Turkish, Persian, Arabian and Hebrew. And so the action of the Militia will reach one thousand million readers, one half of the inhabitants of the globe . . . "

At this time, the printing amounted to only ten thousand copies. Voluntary hawkers went about the country and solicited more subscribers, offering free copies and asking in exchange the visiting cards of the Japanese. The extreme courtesy of the Japanese forbids all disturbing interference in their private lives. Even to send an announcement requires the authorization of the receiver.

Reception was sympathetic, sometimes even enthusiastic. Japan had been dying of spiritual emptiness due to the abandonment of her ancestral faith for an unbridled, atheistic nationalism imported from foreign shores. The disease was spreading, especially in intellectual circles.

With his usual perspicacity, Father Maximilian immediately touched the nerve center. The hunger of these souls had to be satisfied; the uneasiness of these hearts called for a doctor. This was the hour for the missionary. "What an abundant harvest awaits us," he cried, "if we Christians only live our Faith! Words do not impress them, but example does!"

Contacts were set up, no one knows how. The little group of Polish friars, so absolutely disinterested and so happy in their extreme destitution, intrigued, moved, attracted the Japanese. The little review, so humble and so rich in substance, did the rest. The Immaculata served as a magnet. These pagans respected her and learned to love her. The example of these foreigners, who were entirely and passionatly devoted to her service, was truly too contagious. Very fine observers, the Japanese tried to trace such great heroism back to its source.

We have before us a photograph inscribed: "Father Maximilian among the Bonzes." His emaciated and smiling face emerges from the midst of a group with inscrutable features. Was it curiosity that had brought them, or rather the irresistible attraction of sanctity? The priest spent long hours explaining to them the truths of Christianity. One of them declared one day that in the future he would admit no one into this bonzery who would not love the "Seibo no Kishi."

Scarcely two months after his arrival in Japan, on June 25, 1930, Father Maximilian was summoned to the Provincial Chapter, which was to be held at Lwow. Obedient as always, he left, but his heart was heavy because there was no one capable of maintaining the gigantic work in his absence.

At the Chapter, the very future of the Japanese Niepokalanow was put to question. The expenses were heavy, and the capitular Fathers discussed the prudence of undertaking such a foolish venture. Father Maximilian followed his usual tactics. Having explained all his arguments and spoken from the abundance of his heart with that communicative flame which was uniquely his, he remained silent, waited, closed his eyes, and, with that well-known gesture, hid his hands under his capuche. In his little watch pocket he held his rosary and very slowly—while his superiors discussed the business, while the fate of his Japanese mission was at stake—he summoned HIS council, reciting innumerable Hail Mary's.

"I did all I could, and now it is certainly your turn, Immaculate Mother!"

He won on all scores and returned to Japan with full power. This time, he travelled through the continent, crossing Siberia. He was greatly upset by his experiences in this immense country from which God is officially banished. Naturally, he travelled third class with the poorest people. At each large station during the interminable journey, there was a rush toward the hot water spigot, the famous *kipiatok,* which was provided for making tea, the only warm beverage available. In the motley group within the overpacked compartments, it was easy to observe people and even to obtain certain confidences.

There was a long stop at Moscow. Did Father Maximilian go to see the dark and tragic mausoleum that encloses the remains of one of the greatest prophets of the new religion? Did he hold a private interview with Lenin? We would like to see him, humble, small, insignificant, with his hands under his capuche praying for the repose of the soul of this great man with the bitter smile, whose sarcophagus in the midst of scarlet draperies seems surrounded with flames.

Russia had haunted him for years. When he was at the sanatorium lying for interminable hours on his couch, he studied Russian. Since then, he had always tried to keep abreast with the atheistic literature published in Russia; he stored it at home in a locked chest. The great dream of his life was to publish his review in Russian. Toward the end of his life, shortly before the war, he made a prediction.

"One day, you will see the statue of the Immaculata in the center of Moscow atop the Kremlin!"

A great many witnesses heard these words, spoken with an accent of tranquil certainty, but only one, Father Pignalberi, one of the "seven founders," gathered this confidence:

"Before this takes place, we must pass through a trial of blood."

*   *   *

When he returned to Japan on August 24, he surveyed with broken heart the ravages caused by his absence. The mission was on the verge of bankruptcy. For one month the review had not been published and it seemed unlikely to appear.

His presence saved everything, and the work even assumed a new scope. At the Provincial Chapter he had just obtained authorization to found a Japanese branch-establishment from Niepokalanow and to open a novitiate for the natives. The problem was to build a house as soon as possible.

Father Maximilian bought land in the outskirts of Nagasaki, on a steep slope which goes down a long ridge in the opposite direction from the city. Everyone criticized him. Had anyone ever thought of building under such conditions? Why turn your back to the city? The priest smiled but remained unconvinced. May 16, 1931 he opened his Japanese Niepokalanow.

After the cataclysm of the atomic bomb, Mugenzai no Sono—translated "The Garden of the Immaculata"—remained almost intact, because it was protected by the ridge. Only the window panes were blown out; no one was killed in the precincts of the friary. Then, and only then, did they understand.

The original structure of Mugenzai no Sono was, of course, built by the friars themselves. This was a difficult stage. Father Maximilian had hardly any co-workers of his own stature and enthusiasm, or of his spirit of abnegation. Many became discouraged. Many grew homesick and asked to return to Poland. Many were very willing to be missionaries, but elsewhere. We must admit that Father Maximilian did wonders, but nothing came easily to him and each day of

128

his life was a testing crucible for his faith. Most of the time he was "hoping against hope." The heart-rending correspondence of these years says a great deal. Herein he reports to his Provincial, in the name of holy obedience and without the shadow of bitterness, the denials, the treasons, the cowardice of unfaithful brothers.

Fortunately, there were very many who remained faithful. The works of God exhibit a wonderful process of selection; for every one who deserted in discouragement, two others climbed to the front. Opposed to so much cowardice was the silent barrage of sheer heroism. In spite of all difficulties, the house was built, the printing increased, and the "dear pagans" came in ever-increasing numbers seeking light and joy.

Some of the Japanese wrote touching letters. Perhaps in the future someone will publish this correspondence, which reveals the deep nostalgia of the Japanese soul completely open to the message of Christ.

"Thank you for sending me the *Kishi no Sono*. I read it with joy," writes Inohaha Mamoe. "Thank you also for your kind letter. I have been sick for some time. But since my friend, who subscribes to your review, spoke to me of the Catholic religion, I have forgotten my own sufferings."

"It is a great joy," writes N. Masako, "that all of you over there at Mugenzai no Sono work for the glory of God and propagate love for the Immaculata. I am not yet baptized, because my father and mother are opposed to it. Some time ago, I went to Hokkaido, where I met a friend, Kanatsu, who was a member of the M.I. and a reader of the review. I came to know that noble soul, and the priest at Osaka appreciated him very much also. One year has passed since I came back from Osaka. In February of 1933, Kanatsu died. His preparation for death was very beautiful. I admired his trust in God and the Immaculata. When he knew he was going to die, realizing that he would be unable to receive either holy viaticum or extreme unction in his home, he dragged himself to the church, and there the last rites were administered. Not everyone would be capable of such courage! During his last agony, neither his father nor his mother was with him—only the priest and the hospital nurse. Kanatsu loved the Blessed Virgin very much and often asked her to intercede for him. He often urged me also to love her and he never grew tired of repeating to me: 'Pray to the Immaculata! Pray to the Immaculata! Pray to the Immaculata!' Then I tried to follow his instructions and I exhorted others to do the same thing."

"If you had not come to Japan," another declared, "I, Amaki, would still be a pagan."

And here is a gratifying story of conversion. "One day, by chance, an issue of your review fell into my hands and I read the story of the nun who works at Madagascar among the lepers. An American who visiting the hospital said to her, 'I would not like to work here, even if they paid me $20,000.' 'And I,' answered the nun, 'I would not do it for even $100,000, because I work only for love of the Good Lord.' This story impressed me and I began to think. Since that time, I have received your review regularly. In reading it carefully, I learned that if man has sinned and if he repents of his sin and asks the Good Lord for forgiveness through the intercession of the Immaculata, the Lord then forgives him. I used to think that it was sufficient to have killed no one in order to avoid going to hell, but I see now from reading *The Knight of the Immaculata* that this is not enough. We must have faith and pray. Little by little, I instructed myself by reading your review. In October last year, I was baptized and they named me Theresa. And now I have the joy of being a child of God!"

In short, the *Kishi no Sono* served as a course in Christian doctrine, adorned with examples and stories. Its extraordinarily wide circulation, which quickly exceeded the record of former printings, proved the Immaculata to be a sovereignly effective "master-key."

Two years after the foundation in Japan in 1930, Father Maximilian embarked to establish a new Niepokalanow in India. He was exhausted and had attacks of fever, but paid no attention to the state of his health. Had not experience taught him that "the works of God are done only on the Cross"?

"I believe," he writes during this voyage, "that the Blessed Virgin gives each one of us the graces necessary to carry out her plans. Therefore . . . But my pen must not carry me too far. I believe that a local Niepokalanow is to spring up in every country to enable the Immaculata to radiate on every region, using all the productions of modern technical science. We must move quickly. There is no time to lose!"

Landing at Singapore, Father Maximilian once again took up the project of a Malayan review and very discreetly prepared the groundwork. Having arrived in India, he went to Ernakulam, the residence of the Catholic Archbishop. He was received coldly and with suspicion. What could this stranger want? The priest turned to prayer and called upon Saint Thérèse of Lisieux. Had he not agreed with her long ago in Rome that he would pray each day for her canonization if, in return, she would be the patroness of his work? Standing before her statue in a corridor of the archbishopric, he spoke to his little Saint.

"Let us see, little Sister, if you remember."

"A that moment," he writes, "a flower fell at my feet; it was like a rose. Very simply it had detached itself from a vase of flowers at the foot of the statue. This made a definite impression on me and I thought: 'We will see what that signifies.' "

All the correspondence of Father Maximilian is written with this transparent simplicity. He spoke as he wrote, expressing very precisely all he thought. This brought him some enemies and much misunderstanding. He had the soul of a child, incapable of rancor or bitterness. The supernatural was his habitual climate to such a point that he was disconcerting. One could not grow accustomed to his way of talking about saints and especially about the Blessed Virgin, for he referred to them as living persons with whom he familiarly associated. This great realist was not of this earth, and perhaps that is the reason he had such a quality of leadership among human beings in their activties.

Little Saint Thérèse kept her bargain. All the difficulties with the ecclesiastical authorities in India cleared away as if by a miracle, and the Archbishop of Ernakulam wrote to the General of the Order, officially inviting the Polish missionaries.

Unfortunately, preparations were toilsome and Father Maximilian was not there to hasten them. The friars delayed at the sight of the clouds piling on the horizon. War came, and to this day the Polish Franciscans have not again taken up the gauntlet—or the rose—that the little Thérèse had offered to her brother-missionary with such a charming gesture. But the work has only been delayed, for now from the height of heaven they are co-workers, "using both hands" for their missionaries.

Father Maximilian had worked too hard and his health suffered serious effects. On May 23, 1936, he left for Poland, where, at the Provincial Chapter, he was elected Guardian of Niepokalanow in Poland. In spite of all, this was a blow to him. His heart remained with his "dear pagans," and he hoped so much that he would one day find his desired martyrdom over there.

He did not discuss it, however. This was surely the time for heroic obedience. Through the lips of his superiors, the Immaculata had spoken. If he did not understand, so much the better. It was sufficient for him to serve blindly, with all his heart.

Father Maximilian, set your mind at ease. More challenging combats await you.

13

Preparing for the Trial of Blood

THE PRICE OF DEATH IS A LIFETIME

After Father Maximilian's return to Poland a new note was struck in his conferences and writings: the premonition of approaching catastrophe and of his own death.

He had to make the most of the precious time yet left to him. He outdid himself; he was in a hurry! He must save every minute as a miser saves a penny. During the three years preceding the war, all his works took a dizzy swing. On December 8th, the year of his return, he announced the "General Rules of Niepokalanow" designed to bring about even greater order and efficiency. In 1937 he initiated the first 5-year plan of apostolic work. In 1938 "The Small Knight" and the "Little Knight" began publication for young people and children. "The Little Journal" was issued in 11 daily editions.

On December 8th he opened SP3RN—Polish Station 3 Radio Niepokalanow. The same year he began "Miles Immaculatae," the Latin quarterly for priests. In May, 1939 he went to Lithuania to take preliminary steps for establishing a Lithuanian Niepokalanow in Linkiewies. He sent a delegation to Belgium for the same reason. Petitions were coming in from Southeastern Europe, Brazil and elsewhere asking him to establish new Niepokalanows there. The membership in the M.I. approached one million members!

And yet in the midst of all this Father Maximilian emphasized with insistence as never before the supremacy of the spiritual. He wanted to put his "dear little children" on guard against the smoke screen of material success, which is nothing and which does not count if it is not on a par with a superabundant inner life.

This was the secret of his wonderful success. A formidable realist and businessman beyond compare, a marvel to the best technicians, Father Maximilian never permitted himself to be caught in the trap of "efficiency," of statistics and figures. This man, who did not allow himself a minute's rest, defended jealously "the inalienable rights of God to our time," and in offering it to Him he wished to offer also its best fruits.

At Niepokalanow, the atmosphere of prayer and silence strikes the visitor much more forcibly than the powerful presses and the impressive output of this industrial city. One can feel there that at every instant activity is elevated and consecrated by a spirit of love. These workmen are destined to sing with their machines and their tools the praises of the Lord God and of His very dear Mother. The whole enterprise is a liturgy.

It is not *quantity* that counts, but *quality*. Father Maximilian never failed to insist on this point. Once he wanted to tempt his humble followers and asked, "And now what shall we do?" It was his habit to ask their advice, for this incomparable leader was nothing of a dictator and knew very well that real obedience sanctifies liberty but does not crush it.

One of the friars answered in the heat of excitement: "Double the output!"

Another added, "We will double the output if each one perfects himself."

"Exactly!" Father Maximilian exclaimed with pleasure.

"You have hit the point. If our quality is improved, the quantity will come in addition."

On another occasion the friars questioned him. "Tell us, Father, in what does the true progress of Niepokalanow consist?"

He spoke energetically in response. "Certainly, it is not the expansion of the property that will be a proof of progress, nor new and vast buildings! If we get the latest models of machines, if we make use of all technical improvements and all the discoveries of modern science, it still will not be real progress. If our reviews double and even triple their circulation, that still will not prove real progress.

"Then, what must we have for making progress? Fundamentally, Niepokalanow is not so much our visible and exterior activity, be it inside the cloister or outside the cloister. The real Niepokalanow *is our souls*. All the rest—even skill —is secondary. Progress is spiritual, or it is not progress at all! Therefore, even though it were necessary to suspend our work, even though all members of the Militia abandoned us, even though we had to be dispersed as leaves swept by the autumn wind, we would say, my Brothers, that we are truly progressing if the ideal of Niepokalanow continues to shine in our souls."

As I write these lines, I receive the news that the printing establishment of Niepokalanow has finally undergone "nationalization." This means simply the confiscation and transportation of the machinery. Most certainly, one should avoid using the term "religious persecution." In Poland, as in Hungary and all the other countries behind the Iron Curtain, one refers to these things as "progress," or as "the struggle against the reactionary spirit in the name of true democracy."

Now the sons of Father Maximilian will have to meditate with deeper fervor and better understanding upon the passage quoted above and upon so many others which develop the same thought with the insistence of the Old Testament prophets.

* * *

Long before this time, but especially since his return from Japan, Father Maximilian predicted violent persecution. It is noteworthy that he envisioned persecution not only as a trial but also as a chastisement for our own sins of omission.

In an article written in Latin while he was in Nagasaki, we read a passage which deserves careful reflection: *"(Oportet studere) insimul motus antireligiosos nostrae aetatis, fontes eorum, methodos, effectus etc. distinguendo in talibus motibus quid mali (contineant), quia non est alius efficacior modus ad malum motum extinguendum, quam cognoscere quid boni contineant et applicare statim hoc bonum in causam* nostram. *OMISSIONES CIRCA HOC PRODUXERUNT DEPLORATOS EVENTUS IN MEXICO ET HISPANIA."*

I would post this text in every center of Catholic Action! Here is the translation. "We must study the antireligious movements of our time, their sources, methods, results and so forth. We must, above all, discern what is good in them and what is bad, for there is no more effective way to fight and conquer an evil movement than to recognize the portion of good that it contains and to apply it immediately to our own cause. Failure in this regard has brought about deplorable consequences in Mexico and in Spain."

We will pass over the awkward and unskillful Latin. All our seminaries, I fear, have the regrettable habit of butchering Cicero—a torture sufficient to constitute his purgatory. And San Teodoro was no exception. Let us, then, ignore the verbal form and fix our minds upon the thought which is so resplendently profound and true. In writing these lines Father Maximilian touched the most acute point of the great evil of our time. Why have we not known how to save IN TIME the golden grain of truth stolen by the Father of Lies? Why have we not known how to restore it to the barns of the Father of Heaven?

This is one confession which is not always pleasant to hear and still less pleasant to make, for we much prefer to assume the role of victim and martyr than that of responsible agent.

*   *   *

How can we reach our highest excellence? Simply by becoming *saints*. On this point, Father Maximilian was uncompromising.

"*I demand* that you become saints, *and very great saints!*"

"But look here, Father, do you not ask too much?"

"Why, no," he answered. "Sanctity is not a luxury, but a simple duty. It is one of Christ's first principles: 'Be ye perfect as your heavenly Father is perfect.' I will show you that it is not difficult. Have you a piece of chalk?"

Speechless, they stared at him.

Father Maximilian smiled and continued. "It is a question of simple calculation. In a second, I shall put the formula for sanctity on the blackboard for you. You will see how simple it is!"

Calm and grave, he wrote on the blackboard before the wide-eyed young listeners: $v = V$.

"Here is my formula. Do you understand it? The small v is *my* will; the capital V is the will of God. When opposed, they cross like this: $+$, then there is the cross. If you want to cancel out that cross, unite your will and the will of God, who *wants* you to become saints. It is so simple; the one requisite is to obey!"

I remarked at the very beginning of this book that saints are inconvenient to live with and that we should pity the poor sand crabs who race with the eagles. The little formula of

Father Maximilian, which he called "so simple" and for years applied with the ease of a game, is really the quintessence of the greatest books on spirituality and the supreme stake of the whole inner life. The greatest saints alone have succeeded in "cancelling out the cross" and consenting to the most radical renunciation of self. Saint John of the Cross would have delighted in reading these words of Father Maximilian.

We see at a glance that he has not said everything, but we can easily fill in the gap. It is all "so simple," because we belong to the Immaculata, absolutely, unconditionally. Our sanctification is her business and, I would dare say, her specialty. Is she not the Mother of Christ, both Head and members? Then, whoever accedes to her rights over us consents at the same time to the divine invasion, as in those ancient formularies of baptism wherein the catechumen responded: *Consentio tibi, Christe*—"Christ, I surrender to you." Consequently, there will be a direct proportion between the number of souls entirely devoted to the service of the Immaculata and the number of truly heroic saints. On this point, Father Maximilian declares: "THERE IS NOT ONE SINGLE HEROIC ACT THAT WE ARE UNABLE TO ACCOMPLISH WITH THE HELP OF THE IMMACULATA."

In the same conference, he adds: "We must show by very splendid example how to sacrifice ourselves without limits for her. This life is brief; like misers we must take advantage of the little time that remains to us . . . What will be the criterion of our perfection? To do all things as she would have done them in our place—and especially to love God as she loves Him, with her own heart . . . "

Indeed these are things that one cannot learn in books! Father Maximilian does not cease to remind us of this fact. *"These things are learned only on one's knees."*

He preached much more by example than by words. His life was a continual prayer. How I regret that I am unable to quote all the *Fioretti* which I have at hand, with just a trace of their faint and delightful freshness as they come from the rather inexpert hand of some friar who records them.

When there was something important to undertake and a foreman of a section would come to ask his advice, both of them would first kneel down in front of the desk where the Immaculata presided, and only after that would they consider the technical question.

One day, when the exasperating campaign against the *Little Journal* was at its height and malicious reports were falling thick, the editor-in-chief of the newspaper sent a friar to Father Maximilian for an article answering the accusations. A moment later he sent the friar back with a written message that amazed the others: "Let us be led by the Immaculata, let her do what she wants. Gently, my sons, gently; we could bungle everything by acting too hastily."

When they were undertaking a publicity campaign, he repeatedly endlessly, "Remember, my Brothers, that the point is not at all to win subscribers, but to win souls."

At the beginning of each new publication, his adversaries would make the most somber predictions—for instance, that the whole idea was so contrary to common sense that the magazine could not possibly succeed. But they had to surrender in face of the facts. A Polish Franciscan Father explained the fabulous and unforeseen success in this manner: "You can't help it! Before sending off a number, Father Maximilian wraps it so well with prayers that it runs smoothly by itself."

* * *

Aware that the end of his life was approaching, Father Maximilian wanted to leave his "beloved sons" his testament. One day during the octave of the Epiphany, according to an old Polish custom, the friars at Niepokalanow were staging one of the traditional mystery plays of the Nativity, the famous *Jaselka.* After the evening meal, Father Maximilian made an announcement.

"Those of you who wish may stay behind with me."

"I wanted very much to go see the *Jaselka,*" the brother chronicler confides to us, "but even so I stayed."

The little group surrounded the priest.

"Be seated close to me, my sons."

In his voice and on his face there was a certain solemnity commingled with a great sweetness.

"My dear Brothers, for the present I am still with you. You love me and I love you in return. However, you must realize that I will not be here always. I will die, and you will stay. Before departing, I would like to leave you something. Desiring to do only what the Immaculata wants, I said that only those who wished it should stay behind in order that she herself might choose you.

"You call me Father Guardian, and you do right, because I am so. You call me Father Director, and that is correct, because I am the director of these publications. And so I am Father Guardian, Director, Superior. But what am I really? I am your Father, really and truly, even more than your carnal fathers. For through the father of the body God gave you physical life, but from me you have received the spiritual life, the divine life, your religious vocation. Is that not so?"

"Oh yes, Father, undoubtedly. Without you, without *The Knight,* without Niepokalanow, we would not be in the Order!"

And each one in turn started to recall the beginning of his vocation and what he owed to Father Maximilian.

He listened to them with a smile. "Therefore, I am really your Father. Moreover, this is the reason I use familiar, intimate terms when I speak to you, for you are my children."

There was a moment of silence. Father Maximilian held his hands as usual under his capuche, as if he were hiding there some wonderful surprise. Then he began to speak again very shyly. "My children, you are well aware that I am very much older than you and that I will not always be here. That is why I would like to leave you something, to tell you something. May I do so?"

"By all means, Father. Tell us!" And they crowded closer around him.

Visibly moved with emotion, Father Maximilian went on.

"If you knew, my dear Brothers, how happy I am! My heart overflows with happiness and peace, as much as one is able to be happy on this earth. In spite of the troubles and anxieties of daily life, somewhere, at the bottom of my heart, there is always this peace, this joy that cannot be expressed in human words . . . "

He was silent for a moment, and then he continued in a very low voice.

"My Brothers, love the Immaculata, love the Immaculata. She will make you happy. Give her your confidence, give yourself to her totally, without limits. Not everyone is privileged to understand the Immaculata; it is given only to those who ask for this grace on bended knee. The Immaculata is the 'Mother of God.' Do you understand what it means to say 'Mother of God'? Really, truly MOTHER OF GOD! Only the Holy Spirit is able to make known His spouse to whomever and however He wills. I would like to tell you one more thing . . . but I think this is enough."

According to the friar who tells this incident, Father Maximilian gazed at them as though he feared something. The friars earnestly begged him to speak and to keep nothing from them.

"I told you, my Brothers, that I am very happy and that my soul is flooded with joy. Do you know why? *Because heaven has been promised to me in all certitude.* My sons, love the Immaculata, love the Immaculata, love the Immaculata!"

He spoke with such emotion that tears sprang to his eyes and ran freely down his cheeks. There followed a momentary silence that no one except Father Maximilian dared to break.

"There it is, Brothers. That will be sufficient for you . . . "

Their entreaties were touching.

"Speak, Father, perhaps we will never have a similar occasion, nor an opportunity like this."

After a moment's hesitation, he spoke a few words more.

"Since you ask me with such insistence, I will tell you one more thing. *This happened in Japan.* Now, I will tell you nothing more, so do not question me further."

The friars coaxed him in vain to uncover a little more of his secret, but Father Maximilian kept silent, plunged in deep meditation. When they had regained their composure, he spoke very paternally.

"I have disclosed my secret to you in order that it might be a strength and a support in the tests that are ahead of you. There will be sufferings, temptations; perhaps you will be haunted by discouragement. Remember then what I have told you and learn to be ready for the greatest sacrifices, ready for all that the Immaculata will ask of you. My sons, do not desire extraordinary things, but simply to perform the will of the Immaculata, which is the will of God."

Before rising to leave, he added: "You must tell no one what I have just confided to you. As long as I live, say nothing to anyone."

There was so much insistence in his voice that each brother promised.

"It was in Japan . . . Heaven is promised to me in all certitude . . . I am so happy, my heart overflows with peace and joy . . ."

Father Maximilian, you have not said so much since the day your mother wrested from you the secret of the two crowns. This evening's confidence completes the one given in the morning of your life. One would be a very poor psychologist not to understand what you have so clearly unveiled. She herself, the faithful Virgin, must have told you this, so that, humble as you are, you would be convinced of your final perseverance. And was not the rest of the secret, which you would not reveal, a confirmation of the promise of martyrdom? I believe that even the friars who were privileged witnesses did not at first understand the full import of your astonishing revelation. They will understand only little by little, and later.

As catastrophe veered closer, his exhortations became more and more insistent, his allusions more and more obvious. When, at the beginning of 1938, Father Maximilian spoke of war as certain and quite imminent, no one in Europe cared to believe it. He wanted to prepare his brothers, to inure them to the hardships of war. The whole gist of his conferences was such.

"Whatever may happen, all will be for our good, because our condition is such that no one nor anything can do us harm. Exterior and interior sufferings can serve only to sanctify us. Are we not ready to suffer anything for the Immaculata? Suppose they kill us; that will be free passage to heaven! We should even thank our executioners and show our thanks from heaven by obtaining from the Immaculata the grace of their conversion. In short, *we are invincible*.

"And would it not be the supreme honor if we could seal our faith with our blood? Receive as payment for our faithful service a bullet straight to the heart? What a dream! And what happiness to be able to die with the certitude that we have suffered much and worked much for her!"

Sometimes he was even more explicit. His words spoken in March, 1938 were taken down verbatim in shorthand by one of the friars.

"I want you to know, my Brothers, that an atrocious conflict is brewing. We do not know yet what will develop. In our beloved Poland we must expect the worst.

"During the first three centuries, the Church was persecuted. The blood of martyrs watered the seeds of Christianty. Later, when the persecutions ceased, one of the Fathers of the Church deplored the lukewarmness of Christians. He rejoiced when persecution returned. In the same way, we must rejoice in what will happen, for in the midst of trials our zeal will become more ardent. Besides, are we not in the hands of the Blessed Virgin? Is not our most ardently desired ideal to give our lives for her? We live only once. We die only once. Therefore, let it be according to her good pleasure."

One day just before the war, while speaking of the three stages of the spiritual life—preparation for the apostolate, the apostolate, the passion—he said, "As for me, it is only now that I pass to the third stage. Where? How? It is she who knows. What happiness it is to die as a soldier and not as a simple gentleman; not in bed, but on a post of execution, with a bullet right in the heart; to seal our love for the Immaculata with our blood; to pour out the last drop in order to hasten the conquest of the whole world for Christ, through her. That is what I wish for you, my sons, and what I wish for myself . . . '

The harvest is ripe. Let the reaper come—for executioners are necessary to make a martyr! In order to have bread, we must cut the wheat.

14

The Trial of Blood Begins

In September, 1939, the blitzkrieg struck Poland. Squadrons of Junkers flashed through the sky like gigantic vultures. Bombardments followed endlessly one after another, night and day. Villages, hamlets, whole cities flared like torches at the four points of the horizon. The sky, streaked with purple and scarlet, resembled a race track where the horsemen of the Apocalypse gallop their steeds.

The Polish troops fought fiercely to hold the front lines, which cracked on all sides; but they were overwhelmed, encircled, compelled to save, no longer a Poland in sore distress, but the very honor of their country. There were deeds worthy of the Thermopylites, but all in vain.

Each new communiqué announced another mass retreat. Then came a period of silence. Warsaw, the indomitable, still defended itself without hope, amid universal admiration— and universal inertia. The war was lost, and for the soldiers who still fought guerrilla warfare in the forests the only choice was between death and capture. Very many preferred death.

The outrageously humiliated country awoke from its death-like stupor. The ruins continued to smolder; the battlefields resembled charnel houses. Arrogant and well-disciplined by an inhuman *mystique,* the enemy applied methodically, point by point, his plan of extermination. Defeat no longer meant being the captive who groans under the heel of the conqueror, but the condemned who is led to execution by the tyrant. In order that the master race (*Herrenvolk*) hold sway, the slave must serve or die.

Then, throughout the land there was an immense surge of hatred which went to the head like strong wine. The war was lost but not finished. In the forest-underground, the first centers of the Resistance Group were organized. Everyone— men, women and children—took part in the struggle; however, the weapons were different, and therefore it was difficult to find volunteers.

It is so very easy to become intoxicated with hatred, which is like a glass of brandy given to soldiers before attacking with fixed bayonets. Brandy stimulates but does not nourish.

A friend of mine who died a war casualty wrote me one day: *"I hate Germans because they taught me how to hate!"* What a painful confession! To make it, one must have great loyalty and strength of soul. Most of them had no scruples, for hatred seemed just, normal, necessary. At that time, who dared recall the law of perfect charity that covers with its royal mantle even the tyrannical enemy? Forgiving would have seemed shameful. The perversion of the very virtues of Christianity was the greatest crime of the war. Only the saints resist its poison. But we are not saints; only poor sinners, who, when slapped on the right cheek, instead of turning the left, return the slap with a resounding blow.

In the process of Joan of Arc's canonization, special commendation was given the fact that the Maid of Orleans, who knew how to fight and conquer on the field of battle, considered it by far the most difficult of all her grand victories that *she never knew hatred*. The hero of our story, in whose veins ran soldier's blood, resembled her on this point. *Father Maximilian did not know hatred.*

To live in an atmosphere of hatred and not to be contaminated by that hatred is as miraculous as raising the dead to life. One would need to have lived in the brutally battered Poland of those times, to have been humiliated at every turn, and touched to the quick in matters of human dignity and most sacred rights in order to comprehend the full meaning of such a statement. To forgive tyrants while pinned to the Cross, one has to be either Christ Himself or else entirely emptied of self through Him: *"It is no longer I that live, but Christ lives in me."** It is completely above and beyond *human* power.

If we have not believed his words, let us now look at the works of this extraordinary man. Father Maximilian had a soldier's blood and he therefore waged war. His Lady's war. And he cast on the scales more than his life!

From the beginning, Niepokalanow was violently bombarded. Seeing the situation grow graver from hour to hour, Father Maximilian called the brothers together and told them that they could—in fact, must—take refuge with their families, where they would be in less danger. He allowed those who seemed best conditioned to war to stay, for they had begged to remain with him. As for the others, he dismissed them as a father does his children; he blessed them and watched them depart one by one.

Remaining with the little flock—his preferred ones, his staff—he exhorted them to renew their act of unconditional consecration, surrendering to the Immaculata their life and their death. Then he gave them the general absolution and held out a small indulgenced cross for each one to kiss.

Bombardments followed in rapid succession, especially at night. The brothers stayed in the bomb shelters, but Father Maximilian scarcely ever went down. "It seemed," one of them said, "that he did not know fear." All noticed his

---

*Galations 2, 20.

composure, his even temper, his fearlessness. He thought only of his "sons." Later on, when they returned to the dormitories, he would often go to see them at night, to be sure they were all there, no one missing. Even before the war, they were accustomed to these nightly rounds and wondered how he could live with so little sleep.

On September 19, the first German motorcycles appeared. Some S.S. men came to the door of the friary and one of them barked, *Alle raus!* The assembled friars were ordered to vacate the premises immediately. To attend the infirmary, where there were a number of wounded, two were to stay: the brother infirmarian—and who will the other be?

"Father, stay," cried a pleading voice.

"No, my child," he answered gently, "Brother Cyriacus will be more useful." And the priest left with the group.

On the way, some women watching them pass by under convoy began to weep.

"Do not speak to them," Father Maximilian cautioned, "in order not to grieve them more and expose them to reprisals."

He took advantage of the first halt to speak to the friars. "Courage, my sons. Do you not see that we are leaving *on a mission?* They pay our fare in the bargain. What a piece of good luck! The thing to do now is to pray well in order to win as many souls as possible. Let us, then, tell the Blessed Virgin that we are content, and that she can do with us anything she wishes."

The Nazis crammed them into trucks, then into livestock wagons. On September 21, they landed at the camp of Amtitz. It was not yet a concentration camp with all its horror, but it was sufficiently like one to try the most courageous. Ill treatment, taunts of all sorts, painful lack of privacy, hunger and cold. Very soon the "little brothers" began to wonder how long they could hold out. Father Maximilian, ill himself and much more exhausted than the others, revived them, encouraged them, made them pray—and laugh. Incomparable leader, he knew well that sometimes a witty remark is as good as a piece of bread. He distributed peace and joy liberally; his presence itself was a balm.

The Germans were perplexed by this sickly Franciscan who smiled at them and graciously offered them, of all things, medals! They wondered if he was ridiculing them. No, they had only to look at him to be sure. But then? Almost against their wills they softened. Then came his greatest victory.

The German administrator's wife, touched by some gracious trait of the priest, sent him a personal gift—a handsome cake. Father Maximilian, of course, gathered together all the brothers and directed them to cut it into equal parts. Each was given a very thing symbolic slice. At another time, he received a little cream cheese. Lacking plates, he portioned out a teaspoonful into the cupped hand of each brother.

On his feast day, October 12, the brothers extended their good wishes, and Father Maximilian made a little speech.

"This morning I asked myself what I should give you for my feast. Well, here it is. I want you to belong even more to the Blessed Virgin, each day more profoundly. When suffering is far away, we feel that we are ready for everything. Now that we have the occasion to suffer, let us take advantage of it to gain souls. Let us try. Let us try to win as many souls as possible for the cause of the Immaculata."

The prisoners had not been permitted to bring spare clothing. The filth of the barracks was repulsive. It was eaten up with vermin. But even in these unhallowed surroundings, the brothers who woke during the night often saw the thin silhouette of Father Maximilian kneeling on his bed of straw.

When the priest saw that more and more of the civilian

prisoners in the camp were dying, he said to his friars, "Let us make a bargain with the Blessed Virgin. Let us say to her: 'Sweetest Mother, through love I resign myself to remain in this revolting camp, provided the others are permitted to go home. I will remain here to suffer forgotten, despised, alone. I give myself to you to die on this filthy pallet, surrounded by completely insensible and cold hearts . . . ' "

If his "little flock" repeated these words from the tips of their tongues without completely understanding them, he, however, knew well what he was asking!

In spite of all the privations and nagging, the camp of Amtitz was not a "concentration hell." They were hungry, but not dying from hunger. And the friars from Niepokalanow could even observe their Rule, to a certain extent. Father Maximilian often gave them religious conferences. One day he talked to them of Lourdes, of La Salette, and the Blessed Virgin's repeated appeal for penance. "We live in a time of great penance. Let us at least know how to profit by it. Suffering is good and sweet to him who accepts it willingly."

He must surely have realized that not all of his sons were mature enough for martyrdom. What occurred during his long, silent meditations on the reeking and verminous straw of his bed? One day he announced to the friars: "Courage, my children! Our mission is coming to an end. Let us learn how to profit from these last days."

I have before me several testimonies from his fellow prisoners. How I would like to quote them in their entirety! All insist on his heroic and untiring charity. The unpolished style of these accounts makes them all the more touching. Here is a sample, related by Brother Juraszek.

"For a while, my bed was beside his. I awoke during the night once, suddenly aware that someone was very gently tucking in my feet. I opened my eyes—and what did I see?

It was Father Maximilian, who was covering my feet so tenderly. Every time I recall this incident, tears well up. He seemed to me then as infinitely good and tender as a mother. After this, I also noticed that he was secretly giving a large part of his ration of bread to a friar who suffered from hunger more than the rest of us. And our rations were so small that only one with a most loving heart would deprive himself of any part of them."

Another writes: "I cannot find words to express what Father Maximilian was to us in those days of suffering, misery and privation. We must thank the Blessed Virgin for them, because they were very precious moments for us."

The prediction of Father Maximilian was fulfilled to the letter. They were liberated on the very feast of the Immaculate Conception. Had he prayed, as did Christ, that no one of those entrusted to him would be lost? All returned to Niepokalanow, which had been ransacked and plundered but not destroyed. Father Maximilian had no illusions; he was now merely waiting his turn. He did not wish to lose one minute of the precious time that was left for him.

He started by introducing perpetual adoration, in order to increase his "active forces of prayer." Day and night, the brothers succeeded each other before the modest altar. Never before had they prayed with so much fervor.

Gradually they came back from exile. At this time they numbered two hundred and soon reached three hundred and seventy. Unfortunately, many were sought by the Gestapo and could not return. The editorial staff was especially implicated and was forced to remain in hiding. Father Maximilian exerted limitless care to keep in touch with them by means of circular letters, which were priceless.

He exhorted them not only to be patient but also to make new conquests. "Because," he says, "where a soul is perfectly consecrated to the Blessed Virgin, loving her with its whole heart, then it can only be that this perfect love will reflect on its environment, saving many souls."

Therefore, these "separated brothers" should consider themselves on a mission and carry the ideal of Niepokalanow every place they go. "Let us have no truce in our missionary work. Let us spread its influence in every heart. For that purpose let us offer all our troubles and all our sufferings. Let us desire only that the Immaculata be satisfied with us; let us try to make her happy at our expense, whatever the cost.

"How many souls will again find the light, thanks to your dispersion!

"Let us pray, accepting lovingly all crosses, and loving all our fellowmen with no exception, friends and enemies.

"God is love. And as the effect must resemble the cause, all creation lives for love. Not only for the last end, but also for intermediate ends and in all sound and normal action, love is the principal energy and the principal motive force."

When he wrote these lines did he have in mind the famous text of Dante: *Colui che tutto move?** His soul towered so transcendently above all contingent things that we find it difficult to follow him.

But this contemplative was also an apostle and, therefore, a man of action. He would attempt the impossible and publish his beloved review under German domination. After endless red tape, he finally succeeded in obtaining the necessary authorization for a single issue, which appeared on the feast of the Immaculate Conception in 1940. In it Father Maximilian published his last article. He wrote: "If good consists in the love of God and in all that springs from love, evil in its substance is a negation of love . . . "

This is the real conflict. His Lady's war. Above and beyond armies locked in combat, above and beyond violent

---

*"The one who moves all things." **Il Paradiso**, XXIV, 131.

passions and mass slaughter and extermination camps, there are two implacable adversaries at the bottom of each human soul: good and evil, sin and love. And of what use are victories on the battlefield if within ourselves we suffer defeat?

Father Maximilian prepared himself for his supreme battle, a combat of love in the name of Love and for the sake of Love.

15

The Death Camp

In his final article Father Maximilian wrote: "No one in the world can alter the truth. All that we can do is to seek it, find it, and live it."

Here he touched the crucial point. Does not the conflict that lacerates the modern world reduce itself to a crisis of truth? All reformers would like to change the truth; but the question is simply to *recognize* it as it is, serve it, and love it.

"No one in the world can alter the truth . . . " These words sum up the testament of Father Maximilian. They ought to be written in flaming letters above the chapter of history which God is in process of writing straight and upright over the crooked lines of our treasons. Is not Satan's name the Father of Lies?

Father Maximilian waited. He had known for a long time that he would not survive this war. Bloody war, so often foretold by him before countless witnesses, had actually come. He realized that the clash of arms expressed and disguised a far more serious struggle, one which rends the heart of man, that nest of vipers and whirlpool of light, that hidden source of all war. "Our wrestling is not against flesh and blood!' exclaims St. Paul.* Material forces are not the only powers with which we are at war.

The Master had demonstrated the weapons of combat. Would the servant be greater than the Master? *His Passion continues.*

---

*Ephesians 6, 12.

Father Maximilian once said, "The supreme abandonment of the agony was the crowning work of Jesus." With all his ardent soul this priest aspired toward the same triumph, and only God knows with what pacts and contracts he enlisted Divine Mercy. Like sublime lightning rods, the saints throw themselves between our sinful defilement and the demands of infinite sanctity. In order to untie the hands of Love, they make themselves a prey to His Justice.

Let us not, then, look for the immediate cause of Father Maximilian's arrest, for much has been written on that subject, bewildering us with subtle conjectures. The Nazis did not trouble their consciences to justify their acts in Poland. In their methodical extermination, they followed one principal criterion: liquidate the select ones, the leaders. And Father Maximilian certainly belonged to that then pre-eminently undesirable class. His fate was decided in advance.

On February 17, 1941, a black automobile stopped at the door of the friary. One of the brothers immediately recognized the insignia of the Gestapo and quickly ran to inform Father Maximilian, the Guardian.

"Is it true?" he questioned in a voice tinged with anxiety.

But he quickly regained possession of himself. "All right, my son, I am going. Maria!"

And he went to meet them.

They stood face to face—the frail religious with body wasted by illness and privations, and the five police officers, well-fed and in ruddy good health.

"Praised be Our Lord Jesus Christ." He addressed them politely, according to the Polish custom.

They did not honor him with an answer.

One of them snapped, "Are you Maximilian Kolbe?"

"Yes, I am."

"Then, follow us."

He was arrested with four other priests, of whom only two survived.

Before entering the black car that resembled a hearse, Father Maximilian gazed lovingly for the last time upon the domain of the Immaculata and his dear little flock now pitiably huddled together and inconsolable. In his heart he blessed them and said to the Blessed Virgin, "Since I am going away, you must take my place, dear Mother. Be the guardian of your domain, of all your sheep and all your lambs and even of the poor goats, if there are any. I give them all to you."

The automobile drove away with Father Maximilian, who knew that he would never return.

They were taken at first to Warsaw and committed to the terrible prison of Pawiak, whose very name freezes the blood of the Poles in their veins. This was a period of horror, for the Germans were "mopping up" before the invasion of Russia. Thousands of Poles were shot each day. The number was so great that the condemned could not be counted.

Father Maximilian found himself in cell 103. It did not take an hour for him to win every heart. He listened to the confidences of his prison mates, who were enfeebled by the atrocious tortures. He heard their confessions, prayed for them and with them, and treated them as a loving mother cares for her children.

Then came inspection. At the sight of the priest's Franciscan habit, the S.S. group leader was seized with rage. With bloodshot eyes and foam at the lips, he seized the rosary that Father Maximilian wore on his cord and pulled it violently.

"Imbecile, idiot, filthy priest, tell me if you believe in that." And he held up the crucifix of the rosary.

"Yes, I believe," said Father Maximilian in a strong, calm voice.

He was dealt a violent blow in the face. Then another. He doubled up with pain and felt the salty taste of blood in his mouth.

"Well, do you still believe?" sneered the officer.

"Oh! yes, I believe."

Another blow. A shower of blows accompanied by oaths. The poor priest's face turned white, then purple. After each blow he arose again with increasing difficulty, but he continued to face his assailant.

"And now will you tell me that you still believe?"

"Yes, I do believe."

The fury of the officer was unleashed. He struck with all his strength, with closed fists. Father Maximilian sank to the floor, and his tormentor kicked him about. His wild face no longer looked human. Finally, seeing that his victim did not move, he ran off, slamming the door.

Father Maximilian scarcely regained consciousness before doing all he could to calm his companions. His face was horribly swollen. He spoke with great difficulty.

"My friends, you ought to rejoice with me; it is for souls, for the Immaculata!"

The prison doctors took advantage of this incident to transfer Father Maximilian to the infirmary, where at least he was safe from further attack by the diabolical chief.

Meanwhile, the friars at Niepokalanow lost no time. Twenty brothers offered themselves as hostages to replace Father Maximilian. But the Nazis were tenacious of their prey; they refused. The priest could write to his brothers only very rarely and very briefly on postal cards that passed through a rigid censorsip. Among the messages of practical nature, he wrote, "Send us handkerchiefs, and tooth brushes, a civilian suit and food packages addressed by our family names." In these messages he succeeded in inserting some clear and beautiful thoughts drawn from the very depths of his heart.

"The Immaculata, our most loving Mother, has always surrounded us with tenderness and will watch us always. . . . "

"Why worry, my sons, since no evil can strike us unless God and the Immaculata know it and allow it?'

"Let us be more and more completely led by her, wherever and in whatever may be her good pleasure, so that fulfilling our duty to the utmost we may through love save ALL souls. . . . " His last letter, dated May 12, concluded with these words.

A few days later, he found himself on the list of the convoy destined for Oswiecim. They called it "Death Camp" and the name was indeed well chosen.

As Oswiecim, called Auschwitz by the Germans, more than five million condemned men met death after atrocious tortures. The "scientifically" organized crematories were smoking night and day, and a special commission was put in charge of expediting the operation. Each year marked greater progress in the methods of extermination. Whoever entered into this dark enclosure abandoned at the entrance all human hope.

Much, perhaps too much, has been written about the concentration camps, but there remain pages that will never be written on this earth. Words skirt two equally indescribable gulfs: what is beyond and what is below man. Both surpass expression. For if there is a supernatural world above, there is also a supernatural one here below; and what escapes man's grasp in either sphere cannot be captured in human words.

It is no wonder that those who have escaped from concentration camps disagree with what has been written about those camps. By way of comment, they will tell you that it was not exactly as it has been written. Their experience—

personal, unique—does not coincide with that of others; the same hell has passed through the prism of different souls. Here again the profound adage proves itself: "Whatever is received is received according to the capacity of the receiver." It was the same hell, but how can we believe that in this black abyss certain souls may have contemplated stars if we ourselves have seen only the night black as pitch? It was the same hell, but some have known how to make it a springboard for magnificent spiritual ascents. If we do not understand, let us at least take it on faith.

Some unfortunate ones died in revolt and hatred. The revolt was understandable; the hatred natural. There were involuntary martyrs, laborers of the eleventh hour, whose souls suddenly expanded for the acceptance of sacrifice. But there were also conscious victims *who made a business of this blood market,* offering their own blood drop by drop in voluntary holocaust.

Certainly far from being schools of sanctity, these atrocious prisons unchained the worst instincts, even in persons who believed themselves good. Not everyone was able to endure this supreme ordeal that required an entire life's novitiate to face it. Death does not improvise itself!

We have witnessed lamentable downfalls and disgraces which in normal times one would never have believed possible. Faith in the natural goodness of man was shattered. In this crucible souls were revealed for what they were—criminals, monsters, the vast majority of the mediocre; but also some saints. The latter were those men and women who consciously and willingly gave themselves in holocaust to perpetuate the Cross by that act of highest freedom which espouses the divine will. Grace was not excluded from this hell, and who will dare to draw up the balance sheet of its victories?

Hunger, ceaseless and gnawing hunger, tore the entrails

and prevented sleep. Cold made one shiver night and day. There was no end to the tormenting. Incalculable crimes against human dignity were a part of a cleverly elaborated program. Before *killing* the victim, they had to *crush* it.

Among these outcasts, priests were ranked next to last, just one category above that reserved for Jewish prisoners. They were commonly called "priest swine," were given the hardest work, and regularly lashed with horsewhips. Humiliated, reduced to tatters, hunted out like beasts by a mysterious hatred, *priest-hatred,* without willing it and even at times without knowing it, they *gave witness.* Their poor faces, swollen and unrecognizable, recalled the face of Christ covered with spittle.

Father Maximilian *willed* it all. Father Maximilian *understood.* In this hell he was one of those rare souls who are supremely free, since, for a long time, there had been no division between his will and the will of God. Like Saint Andrew the Apostle, like the Poor Man of Assisi, he greeted the Cross as his beautiful bride: "O happy Cross!" And he prepared himself for the wedding feast.

He belonged to the company called "Babice," which was treated miserably and had for its superintendent Krott the Bloody. This monster vowed a merciless hatred for Father Maximilian. With his companions, the unfortunate priest had to carry large tree trunks at a quick trot (*laufschritt!*); and each time he fell exhausted under their weight, blows rained hard on his emaciated back. To his comrades, who in deep pity attempted to help him, his unvarying counsel was, "Do not expose yourselves or you will receive the same treatment. The Immaculata helps me. I will hold on."

This veritable way of the Cross lasted two weeks.

One day, Krott spied him scarcely creeping along and seized the opportunity to amuse himself. He himself chose the largest tree trunks and loaded them on the shoulders of the priest with the order, "Run!" Father Maximilian went a few steps, stumbled and collapsed. Then Krott assailed him and began with deliberate aim to kick him unmercifully in the stomach and then in the face.

He howled, "You don't want to work, faker? Wait, I'll show you what work is!"

At meal time he called out Father Maximilian and ordered him to stretch out on a pile of wood. Then the burliest of his butchers laid on fifty lashes. Father Maximilian lay motionless, and Krott pushed him into a rut, covered him with dry branches and left him for dead.

We owe all these details to an eyewitness, Father Szweda, one of the few survivors of Oswiecim.

The companions of the poor priest clenched their fists but could do nothing; the least interference would only aggravate his case. It was only at night after work that they could bring him back, a mass of bloody tatters. The next day, at least, he was exempt from work.

The hospital was a place of terror, where the sick died like flies—three or four on the same bed, without medical care or anyone to attend to them. Father Maximilian chose the worst place, very near the door.

"In this way I see the dead carried out and I can pray for them."

He was the admiration of all in the prison hospital, attendants as well as fellow prisoners. He repeatedly declared, "For Jesus Christ, I am ready to suffer much more. The Immaculata is with me. She helps me."

One evening, the infirmarian secretly brought him a glass of tea, the greatest dream of those who burn with fever. To his astonishment, Father Maximilian flatly refused.

"The others have none, and I would not like to be an exception."

In spite of prohibitions and threats of punishment, he

162

heard confessions all night long. As soon as it became dark, the sick crawled haltingly toward his bed and passed long moments there. A priest who later escaped relates that Father Maximilian "clasped him on his heart as a mother does her child" and whispered the sweet consolation: "Look to the Immaculata. She is the 'Consolation of the Afflicted.' She loves us and listens to us. She helps all of us."

Father Maximilian remained about two weeks in the hospital, then was transferred to the block of the invalids, who were exempt from work but received only half of the meager ration of the camp. Father Maximilian often gave his away, with the simple remark, "You are more hungry than I."

One day, he confided to a young comrade who was doing his utmost to spare him: "No, my son, I will not survive the camp. But you and the other young ones, yes."

In this hell, he was always even-tempered, always gay and full of spirit, cheering the downhearted, rebuking the defeatists. "My children, you MUST hold on. You MUST survive. Entrust yourselves to the Blessed Virgin. She will help you; she will save you."

From time to time, he risked the lash and preached real sermons before an audience of skeletons and dying men. Those of his group who survived remember such a meeting one Sunday when he spoke of "the relationship of the Immaculata to the three Persons of the Holy Trinity" with such burning enthusiasm that even the unbelievers were enraptured by it.

Despite all the efforts of his friends, they could not keep him longer in the block of the invalids, and he was transferred to Block 14, where the supreme test awaited him.

16

The Sunset Was RED

"With Her I Can Do All Things"
Love Stronger Than Death

It was the end of July, 1941. In Block 14, the one where they kept Father Maximilian, a prisoner was missing. Another escape! The prisoners recalled with terror the threat of Fritsch, the chief officer, that for every fugitive twenty men of his block would be condemned to death by STARVATION.

That night, no one in the barracks slept. A mortal fear seized these wretched men broken down by most refined torture, who often longed for death as a release.

Death, yes! But not *that* death which is the most dreadful of all. To fall under the executioner's bullet, to die a soldier's death did not frighten these brave men. They could face the gallows without trembling. But to be in agony for days, dying by slow degrees amid inexpressible tortures that dry up the entrails, fill the veins with fire, lead to madness . . . ! Merely to think of these things froze their blood, and they felt themselves overwhelmed by indescribable terror.

Throughout the camp, tales were told of the horrifying happenings in the Block of Death. Sometimes at night the howlings of wild beasts resounded from this place of terror.

Those condemned to starvation, they say, scarcely resembled human beings and even frightened the guards; for the agony consists not solely of *hunger* but of torments of *thirst* as well. During his famous hunger strikes, Gandhi drank liquids. Death from hunger, as long as one can drink, is not unbearable. It is the thirst that is inexpressible torture.

Each of the prisoners asked himself, "And what if it is I?" These heroes of the Resistance Movement wept like little children. To a young boy trembling at his side Father Maximilian whispered, "Are you afraid, my child? Don't be frightened! Death is nothing to be afraid of."

* * *

The next morning at the roll call, the head of the camp announced that the fugitive had not been caught. He gave orders for all the blocks to break ranks—all but Block 14. They stood exposed to the burning sun. Hours passed. It was strictly forbidden to give them anything to drink. Some S.S. officers watched them and "restored order" by beating them with the butts of their guns.

Every now and then, someone collapsed. When blows failed to stir the unconscious and insensible victims, the executioners dragged them out of the lines and piled them in heaps one on top of the other. The ghastly piles grew by the hour. The faces of those who survived were so swollen by the heat that they were unrecognizable.

Father Maximilian, the sick man despaired of twenty times by the doctors, did not faint, did not fall. Like Mary at the foot of the Cross, he remained STANDING.

Had he not repeated a hundred and a thousand times, "With her, *I can do all things*"?

Now was the time to prove it. Here was the moment to set the example! Under the relentless July sun his decision slowly ripened. He had given all. Since this life was no longer for him, was it not the moment to let it be taken? In the profound silence of his soul, in the peace of love at its apex, he listened.

Hours passed. About three o'clock in the afternoon, the officer granted the prisoners a half hour's rest and allowed them to eat some soup. For some, it was their last meal. Then they continued to stand at attention until evening, awaiting the sentence.

The camp commandant, Fritsch, was fond of spectacular gestures. He prided himself on a remarkable sense of pedagogy. What an opportunity to give a lesson! Like an expert animal trainer, he awaited the proper moment. It was the evening roll call. The different blocks returning from work fell into line on the vast marching field. All eyes turned toward the heap of fellow prisoners already put to death. Countless lips moved in silent prayer, and an almost visible terror passed through the long lines.

Commandant Fritsch circled slowly as he listened to the reports; then he suddenly halted in front of Block 14. His head resembled a bulldog's. He visibly delighted in the terror of his victims. There was such a silence that one could hear the buzz of a fly. Suddenly he began to speak, or rather bark. His staccato words cut the deathlike silence one at a time.

"The fugitive has not been found. Ten of you will die for him in the starvation bunker. Next time, twenty will be condemned to death."

He passed down the first line, looked them in the face, seemed to reflect a moment, then snapped in bad Polish: "Open your mouth. Put out your tongue. Show your teeth."

The victim, gasping grotesquely, looked at him like a beast led to the slaughterhouse, while Fritsch appeared to be carefully inspecting his teeth. Was this a method of cruel mental torture, or a health test such as one sees in the horse market? Would he choose the strongest or the most feeble? In the German camps, the principle was to spare those in good health, but Fritsch was a sadist and followed only his caprices. He took enjoyment in passing among these shadows like an angel of death.

At last, he raised his hand and pointed. "This one."

Palitsch, his assistant, immediately wrote down the number on the list of the condemned. At Oswiecim a man was only a number.

Pale as a winding sheet, the man stepped out of line. In the silence, the hiss of breathing sounded like a moan.

Fritsch continued to choose. It amused him.

"This one. That one there. And that one."

There were ten. Ten condemned to death. When falling out of line, one of them cried, "Oh, my poor wife, my poor children, whom I will never see again!"

Those remaining in the ranks breathed again. Only those who have been in a concentration camp know how fiercely one clings to life. At that particular moment, saving one's life consisted in escaping a most horrible death.

Vice-Commandant Palitsch, the tool of Fritsch, yelped a new order. *"Schuhe weg!* Take off your shoes!"

A well-known ritual: those condemned to death go to the place of execution with bare feet. The clatter of wooden shoes thrown to the ground mingled with the sobbing of one of the victims, the same one who a moment ago had bewailed his wife and children.

"Links rum! Turn to the left!"

The host of prisoners watching this inhuman scene shuddered, for "to the left" was the ominous Block 13, with the black wall of execution, the gallows—and the starvation bunkers.

Suddenly, something totally unexpected happened. A prisoner carved out a path through his dumbfounded comrades. He dare to leave the ranks. His head slightly bent to one side, he looked with his large eyes squarely into the face of the speechless Fritsch.

A murmer spread like a wave breaking into foam. Word passed from line to line.

"It is Father Maximilian! Father Kolbe!"

The camp commandant dove for his gun, stepped back a pace, and yelled, "Halt! What does this Polish pig want of me?"

Father Maximilian stood facing him, very calm, a faint smile playing at his mouth. He spoke in such a low voice that only his nearest comrades heard him.

"I would like to die in place of one of the men you have condemned."

Fritsch looked at him stunned. These words surpassed anything he had ever heard. He thought he must be dreaming. He who never listened to an objection, who *never* reversed a decision, who shot down the rebellious with a single bullet, now stood rooted under the clear gaze that unwittingly subdued him, Fritsch, who domineered as lord and master. But at the moment it was Father Maximilian who commanded the situation.

The commandant bewilderedly asked, "And why?"

Did he question out of curiosity or did he wish to regain his self-possession, gain time? He, Fritsch the Bloody, holding discussion with a prisoner!

Father Maximilian was an excellent psychologist. He realized that he must make defeat easy for his executioner. Heroics would spoil everything. It was better to invoke an unwritten paragraph of Nazi law: "Cripples and weaklings must be liquidated.'

He spoke quietly. "I am old and good for nothing. My life will serve no purpose."

"In whose place do you want to die?"

"For this one. He has a wife and children."

The priest pointed to the man who had just bemoaned his fate, Sergeant Gajowniczek.

Except for those standing near by, the great majority of prisoners present at the roll call heard none of this conversation, understood nothing. Their astonishment was boundless. It was the first time that they had ever seen Fritsch talking to a prisoner.

For once, curiosity outstripped his cruelty. Fritsch tried to solve the riddle.

"Who are you?"

The answer came with solemn brevity. "A Catholic priest."

He did not say "religious." He did not say "Franciscan." Nor did he say "member of the M.I."—his humility would have prevented his using the word *founder*. He simply said, "A *priest*." He would die, he wanted to die, *as a priest, because* a priest is endowed with the most august privileges which man may enjoy on this earth; he is the master of the Body and Blood and forgiveness of the Lord. Those on the way to their deaths must not be deprived of the assistance of the priest in their final struggle.

A momentary silence followed. What thoughts ran through the head and heart of Fritsch the Bloody? Did he vaguely suspect that what had transpired was utterly *beyond* him, that heaven had need of him to populate it with a new martyr? He had not the strength to refuse.

Father Maximilian was waiting. His face, now clean-shaven, seemed very young and delicately transparent. He did not look at his executioner. He was seeing much farther. The setting sun enveloped him in purple and gold, and he seemed to officiate in this solemn stillness. Never before, during the roll call, had silence lasted so long.

At last, Fritsch spoke in a hoarse voice. "All right, *Geh mit*. Go with them."

He added neither oath nor insult. From that moment, Fritsch kept silent.

The lips of Father Maximilian moved softly. He was praying. No doubt, Fritsch the Bloody was among those for whom he had, just now, very simply offered his life. Palitsch, the vice-commandant, awaited the decision, pencil in hand. He very efficiently erased one number from the list and wrote another—16670. The formality was so simple: one number replaced another. *But never before had a man reduced to the simple rank of a quantity consummated such a triumph of quality!*

The fiery ball of the sun was poised on the horizon, and the sky flared like an immense monstrance. The witnesses had never beheld so glorious a sunset. Father Maximilian, *the priest,* was going to celebrate his last Mass in the liturgical red of the Common of Martyrs.

Another order rang out, "March!"

Barefoot and clothed only in their shirts, the condemned walked slowly toward the Block of Death. All eyes followed them. Father Maximilian walked at the end of the line, a shepherd behind his flock. His head was slightly bent to one side, and heaven was in his heart.

"My Queen and Mistress, my Mother. Oh, dearest Mother, keep your word! It is for this hour that I was born!"

They advanced, and little by little night descended. Finally, they turned their backs to the sun and walked into the night. To describe this scene with justice, to portray it in detail, would require the pen of a Dante, or the brush of a Rembrandt or a Goya. There are certain silences that make the angels weep.

*   *   *

The guides at Oswiecim never fail to show curious tourists the infamous Block of Death, where thousands of victims have agonized in unspeakable torture. The horrible starvation bunkers are under the ground—dank, dark cells, most of them without windows.

When the condemned of Block 14 arrived there on that unforgettable evening of July, 1941, more than twenty wretched prisoners lay in torment in the next compartment. The thick walls could not deaden their cries, their moans, their screams. The new arrivals were ordered to remove all clothing. Hypnotized by fear, they obeyed like robots. Father Maximilian, however, reflected at that moment that Christ died on the Cross NAKED. He obeyed with full consciousness and with all his love.

This nakedness was a heart-rending humiliation. The tyrants wanted to crush them before they suffered this excruciating death. The prisoners had hitherto managed to preserve a shred of human dignity by means of their tattered, beggarly rags so often spattered with blood. Now they were completely frustrated. But, lamentable flock that they were, shoved and beaten with gun butts into a windowless bunker, without air, without pallets, this flock of men about to die was not without a shepherd. The priest was there, not only to die with them but to help them die.

The heavy door was shut on the black pit filled with sobs. From this moment on, the condemned would receive nothing to eat, nothing to drink. One of the jailers sneered the German saying, "You will dry up like tulips."

The jailers, however, were quick to realize that this time something was changed. Before that day, the starvation bunkers, like miniature hells, had reverberated with the howling of the damned. The first hours and the first days after the closing of the fatal door had plunged them into a frenzy of despair, and only gradual death had succeeded in calming them. But this time they marveled that the condemned did not scream, did not curse. They sang! From the next compartment, where a moment ago there were only cries and screams, feeble voices joined in the singing. This place of torment was transformed into a chapel of fervor, and from cell to cell they answered one another with prayers and hymns.

The jailers looked at each other in amazement and remarked, "Never before have we seen anything like this."

Some writers have tried to fictionize the secret of this closed cell. They have invented sublime dialogues, sparkling conversations, and marvelous deeds, with Father Maximilian, naturally, as the hero and the protagonist. They would have him, like Socrates before his death, take advantage of these last days to instruct, enlighten, and set these souls vibrating in high contemplations.

We, rather, respect silence. In this factual book we have not quoted a single word of Father Maximilian that was not really his, duly certified. We have not related one single fact that had not numerous witnesses to verify it. Let us not try to divine what God has reserved for Himself, what He will reveal one day, on *His* day, the day of judgment, in the most imposing of epics! It is certain that the reality was much more noble and beautiful than anything our short imagination could invent. To understand a saint, it is necessary to be a saint: *Sancta sanctis*. But there are moments when there is only one thing for us to do: be silent and kneel.

Father Maximilian did not die like Socrates, the greatest of men. To die as he did, this priest had to be immensely more than mere man, more than any great man. He needed that divine supplement for which human nature hungers and thirsts more vehemently than for bread and water. For Father Maximilian it was sufficient that he die exactly as Christ did on the Cross.

From these torture chambers converted into a chapel there came voices weakening with each passing day. We have only scant details on what happened *within*. Some few details are supplied by the precious testimony of a prison inmate named Borgowiec, who acted as undertaker, since the S.S. officers would not venture into the pestilential air of those unventilated and sewerless dens. Each morning, Borgowiec entered to remove the corpses. He always found Father Maximilian, either on his knees or standing in the center of the chamber, praying aloud—"even though the others lay like a heap of rags."

The S.S. officers stationed at the door watched the attendant closely so that he could speak very little with the condemned men. His testimony reveals that during those first days they were so completely lost in prayer that they did not hear the door being opened and that only the bellowing of the S.S. men could attract their attention. Later, some wept and begged for a little water; but Father Maximilian was always calm, asked for nothing, and looked at his executioners with a profound serenity. They could not stand his gaze and demanded, "Turn your eyes away. Do not look at us that way!" As they went away, they would mutter among themselves, "We have never seen a man like him."

Here is a rugged detail that will perhaps offend delicate ears. So much the worse! Let us at least be strong enough to *read* what others had to suffer. Borgowiec testifies that although he was supposed to empty the toilet bucket every day, he was spared this drudgery because the bucket was always empty.

*   *   *

Days passed. The prisoners of Oswiecim prayed for the dying. They organized a lookout squad to learn at least the date of their death. It may have been simply a coincidence, but one of the witnesses attested that "the sacrifice of Father Maximilian saved the lives of a great many of the inmates," for the officers, "touched in spite of themselves, did not beat or kill so many during work." The fact is, as all the former prisoners of Oswiecim know very well, that, from the spring of 1941, the hardships in that camp were somewhat mitigated. The older survivors invariably greeted the newcomers with the remark, "Ha, if you had been here in 1940!" I simply state the fact; I do not pronounce on it. Here again, let us cede to judgment day the task of establishing certain relationships between cause and effect. In his bunker of death Father Maximilian prayed *also* for his executioners; it is not at all rash to believe that in some cases he may have been heard.

Days passed. It was the eve of the Assumption. In Father Maximilian's bunker there were only four survivors; of the four, he alone was clearly conscious. He no longer stood nor knelt, but remained seated. He had dismissed his little flock one by one. The last three, stretched out unconscious on the floor, were ready to appear before God. The good shepherd had finished his task. He had earned his rest. Now, and only now, could he die.

At the moment when the jailers entered to finish him, the priest was seated on the floor in a corner, praying. Seeing the hypodermic syringe, he himself stretched forth his fleshless arm for the deadly injection. Borgowiec, who could stand it no longer, fled.

A little later, it was he who was assigned to clean out the bunker. Upon entering, he found Father Maximilian "still seated propped up in the corner, his head slightly bent to the side, his eyes wide open and fixed on one point. As if in ecstasy, his face was serene and radiant." While the other corpses were dirty and had contorted and ravaged faces, "his body was spotless, and one could say that it radiated light."

"I will never forget the impression that this made on me," concluded Borgowiec.

At the news of the priest's death, his comrades wept for him as for a father. They tried in vain to have his body exempted from the implacable law, but he was burned as were all the others in one of the crematories that smoked day and night.

*"Dies Natalis Maximiliani Kolbe: in Vigilia Assumptionis . . . "** The faithful Virgin came to take him on one of her most beautiful days, when the entire Church was making preparations to celebrate her supreme glorification. Would it be foolhardy to believe that she was holding in her hands the two crowns which she had one day long ago allowed him to glimpse: the white—and the red?

*   *   *

I have taken up the gauntlet. I have accepted the challenge. I have kept my imagination firmly bridled, and in this story, often improbable, there is not one word nor one fact that is not *true*.

And now, Pierre, my brother,—and all you numberless others who have shared his despair—do you believe me?

*   *   *

---

*"Birthday of Maximilian Kolbe: the Vigil of the Assumption . . . "—this is the way in which his passing will be recorded in the official Roman Martyrology.

Why His Beatification NOW?

There are always those persons who try to go beyond partisan controversy to read the signs of the times in the light of HIM WHO IS THE LIGHT.

To all such persons, the beatification on October 17, 1971, of Fr. Maximilian Kolbe, scarcely thirty years after his death in a starvation bunker at Oswiecim-Auschwitz, is more than just a grandiose ceremony in Rome's Basilica of St. Peter. It is above all a WARNING and a CALL.

In focusing the attention of the People of God on Father Maximilian, the Church obeys the SPIRIT who governs her through the instrumentality of her responsible authorities, and dramatizes the call of Vatican II for a return to essentials.

We are not just dealing here with another saint officially proclaimed by the Church. We are dealing, in the first place, with an ACT OF WITNESS in the quite near and verifiable past—a witness that cannot be banished comfortably to the limbo of a golden legend.

We are dealing with a LIFE, and even more, with a SURVIVAL: no one throughout the entire organic diversity of the People of God in Poland doubts that the surprising spiritual fruitfulness of that enslaved, humiliated, frequently harrassed Church can be explained only by the bloody labors of so many anonymous victims formed by the spiritual doctrine of Father Maximilian Kolbe.

Through his doctrine they have found the strength not only to "hang on" but to *pardon their executioners,* to *love* them and *pray* for them.

The explosion in vocations which have never dried up, even after a war which cost Poland six million dead, can only be explained by this accumulation of divine energies within the Communion of Saints: we are sharing beings who will not know until the day the Lord comes how marvelously dependent we have been on each other, how much we have given and received from one another.

* * *

What was Fr. Maximilian Kolbe's secret? What is the key to his life and his death?

The response is simple and unquestionable: his love for Our Lady, the Virgin Immaculate. A love not in the least sentimental, but springing up from the depths of theology and the unfathomably rich reservoir of tradition.

This man was endowed with a remarkable scientific spirit. In the world he would have been a ranking inventor (did he not foresee jet airplanes and interplanetary spacecraft?) As such he carried out with faultless fidelity all the implications of a doctrine that he drew, certainly, from the inspiration of thundering graces, but which he always submitted to the supervision of the Church.

He was a man who obeyed without question—following the example of the Virgin who said at the Annunciation, "Let it be done to me as you say." Paradoxically, he made this obedience a springboard: the incredible range of his work is literally borne up on the "yes's" spoken in the night of faith.

Paradox or scandal? We know to what extent the very notion of obedience is today debased, profaned, and held unworthy of "mature men." Decidedly, in 1971, Father Maximilian seems to go at cross currents with history.

The stone over which certain modern Christians, anxious for renewal, stumble is Marian doctrine. For twenty years but especially since the end of Vatican II, we have been watching a real campaign to squelch the Holy Virgin, or at least to put her under a bushel. It is all done with great, good intentions and not without reverence.

As was often the case in the Church's past, this doctrinal and spiritual ostracism justifies itself by claiming Christ will be harmed by the worship given His Mother. Its practitioners start by condemning pious exaggerations no sensible person would think of defending, then proceed to throw the baby out with the bath. I mean they throw out recognized doctrines and practices which both the Catholic Church and all eastern Churches have proclaimed and recommended from the dawn of salvation. In the name of a narrow and "wild" ecumenism they thus undermine the most venerable bonds which unite us to our Orthodox brothers and, let's say it bluntly: *they scandalize them.*

*   *   *

The tree is known by its fruits. Let us put to our readers a simple question: the methodical and progressive elimination of the Virgin Mary from the piety and the attention of the People of God—has it made them more open and more sensitive to Christ? If Marian doctrines and practices were curbs and obstacles, shouldn't we be seeing now a great soaring of Christ-centered theology and spirituality? Right here is where the saddle pinches.

The doctrinal clouding we now witness, the progressive draining of the very notions of *mystery* and *the sacred* of their meaning, the mini-theologies on the "death of God" that find their way into would-be Catholic magazines, the growing confusion of the People of God, especially the little ones and the poor—all this says little in favor of those updated people who believe they build up Christ by pulling down his Mother.

For those who know how to observe it, the drying up of priestly and religious vocations, as also the crisis in the interior life—the famous "horizontalism" that plagues the Church—seems to coincide in certain countries of Europe with the slow but progressive elimination of Marian observances from the official prayer of the Church.

Who does not know this official disinterestedness does not correspond to the desires of and feelings of the POOR, who are the silent depths of the People of God, the "Anawim"—the "degraded," afflicted little people—of the Beatitudes and the Magnificat?

The uneasiness of these humble souls is growing. Well it might, for their needs have been ignored amidst all the high-sounding talk. In their increasingly shabby devotions regarding the Virgin Mary, they have had to rely on their own ideas, which often as not are naïve and disoriented. Those responsible for this breakdown should reflect on that. Never has one spoken as much of the Church of the Poor, and never have the Poor of Yahve been to such a degree shocked and humiliated.

If someone should dare conduct an on-the-scene inquiry regarding this delicate point, he would find the results terrifying. It suffices to point out as an example the fate of the Rosary which has been prohibited in a number of parishes and which some, with a condescending shrug, consider "a devotion for little old ladies" destined to disappear as the Church progresses toward maturity.

The little ones, the poor, the humble *as one* fasten themselves fiercely to forms of Marian devotion redolent of the past. Meanwhile the moat that separates the instigators of certain more or less arbitrary reforms from the living, secret depths of the People of God continues to deepen.

There are those who fulminate against the rapid increase of wondrous events and questionable apparitions attributed to Mary, but do they not realize we are dealing here for the most part with a discharge or pouring out of repressed religious sentiments?

*　　*　　*

Now, in the plan of Salvation, the Virgin Mary is the appointed spokesman of YAHVE'S POOR. "She occupies in the NEW LAW such a place that the believer spontaneously looks forward to discovering in the Old Testament the foreshadowing of her coming, her virtues and her mission." She is the marvelous culmination of a whole line of "POOR ONES," those "ANAWIM" which Yahve recognizes as HIS PEOPLE, whom he glorifies by saving (Psalm 149).

The prayers, the hopes, the obscure expectations of uncountable generations have been concentrated in that woman "who so profoundly identified herself with the spirit of the Anawim that, borne up in the new creation wrought by the Incarnation, she became the most perfect expression of that spirit. She is the echo of a long chain of praying figures; she takes into her spirit all their power to receive the God who comes; she sums up their expectation. . . .

"The Church of the Poor in its immense symphony of prayer was a prelude to the MAGNIFICAT . . . Each of the Anawim prepared for it and announced it . . . In the circle of religious souls who awaited the Kingdom she was the most qualified for that "listening post of the faith" in which St. Paul sees the fundamental attitude of religion (Galatians 3, 2). There was in her heart "a silence, a readiness, a void, an appeal" which was blooming in messianic joy, in the blessedness of the poor." With all the strength of her youth she entered into the mystery of her vocation, accepting forever and ever, by her flawless *"Let it be done,"* her role as

MOTHER of the SON OF GOD, in the fathomless humility of SERVANT.*

This is it, the Immaculate Conception: fulness of grace in the fulness of accepted, glorified, exalted poverty.

Would it be rash to suppose Jesus thought first of his mother when He was proclaiming the priority given the little poor ones at the gates of the Kingdom?

"He trembles with joy under the action of the Holy Spirit and says: I bless you, Father, Lord of heaven and earth, for hiding these things from the learned and the clever and revealing them to the very little ones. Yes, Father, for such has been your good pleasure." (Lk. 10, 21; Mt. 11, 25).

This text has been for two thousand years the great charter of rights for the ANAWIM in the Church of Christ, the narrow gate of which the pharisees of all times and all races know nothing, where the "poor" rush in following the "VIRGIN OF THE POOR," the MOTHER OF GOD.

"Therefore let no one on the basis of some false insight imagine Mary, being a creature, an obstacle to union with our Creator. It is no longer Mary who lives, but Jesus alone, God alone who lives in her. . . . Mary exists for no one but God, and far from keeping any soul for herself, she throws each one onto God. The more perfectly a person is united to her the more perfectly she unites him to God. Mary is God's wonderful echo. She answers, "GOD," whenever anyone cries, "MARY" (St. Grignon de Montfort, *The Secret of Mary*).

* * *

Fr. Maximilian Kolbe is a true offspring of the ANAWIM, a "man of the Beatitudes." He payed the price. It is hard for us fifty years later to grasp all there was of the

*Albert Gelin, LES PAUVRES DE YAHVE, Cerf. 1953, p. 121 and ff. Cf. **Lumen Gentium,** VIII, 55: "She stands out among the poor and humble of the Lord, who confidently hope for and receive salvation from him."

"revolutionary" in his work, how it was a scandal to some, and lunacy to others. He carried the forerunner's cross in the full meaning of the term.

At a time when class difference still played a full part in the discipline of religious life, he fought for equal rights for the "lay brothers" in the name of their irrevocable consecration to the service of God. He thus renewed the spirit of St. Francis of Assisi who was not a priest, and who in his rule battered in the feudal structures of his time. The extraordinary flood of vocations to Niepokalanow demonstrates the degree to which the ideal of the "worker Brother" fascinated the young. *The consecration of one's work became a liturgy.*

On this point, as in so many others Fr. Maxamilian Kolbe was ahead of Vatican II. One could glean from his writings the basic elements of a real *"theology of work,"* not superimposed but inherent in the Christian vocation, "responsible" for the future of the world.

He knew how to get at the root causes of the great temptations of our times, which are spawned by equally great acts of treachery. Attentive to the "signs of the times," he left to his sons as an order, the strict obligation to recover the bits of truth buried in the errors which live off them. Thus deprived of their support these errors will lose their excuse for existing.*

* * *

The Marian doctrine of Fr. Maximilian Kolbe gathers up in a powerful summary the data of Sacred Scripture and

---

*In a letter from Japan, composed in Latin, he wrote: "It is necessary to study the anti-religious movements of our time, their methods, results, and so on. One must especially distinguish what there is in them of good and what there is of evil because there is no more effective way to combat and conquer a bad movement than to recognize what is good in it and apply that immediately to our cause. The sins of omission in this regard have brought tragic consequences in Mexico and in Spain. . . . "

the riches of the most pure tradition. No one has ever been as careful as he to remain faithful to the teachings of the Church. Gifted with charisms and confident in the Immaculata, he jealously guarded the secret of his exceptional graces. He did not betray any but a few odd ends of them a short time before his death, in order to strengthen his children.

His life was a miracle humbly concealed within a game of secondary, more apparent factors. He tried to pass by unnoticed as much as others desire to appear: "I would like," he used to say, "to use myself up completely in the service of the Immaculata, and to disappear without leaving a trace, as the wind carries my ashes to the four corners of the world. . . . "

On that point, as on so many others, he was heard. There are not now, there never will be any "relics" of Fr. Maximilian Kolbe. But isn't he in the process of making a conquest of the globe?

With what joy he would have greeted the Second Vatican Council. It all revolves around pastoral concern—that "hunger for souls" that literally devoured him. The marvelous Chapter VIII of *Lumen Gentium,* dedicated to "MARY, THE BLESSED VIRGIN MOTHER OF GOD, IN THE MYSTERY OF CHRIST AND OF THE CHURCH, sums up in a powerful outline all his Marian teaching.

We know what importance he attached to obedience, his famous formula "v = V," which brings our wills into line with God's in an act of sovereign freedom.

"The Virgin Mary," declares Vatican II, " . . . cooperated in the work of the Savior in an absolutely unequaled way by her OBEDIENCE. . . . That is why she is in the order of grace our MOTHER. . . . Mary's function as mother of men in no way obscures or diminishes this unique mediation of Christ: ON THE CONTRARY IT SHOWS FORTH ITS POWER. . . . She is the MODEL OF THE CHURCH . . .

which brings forth to a new and immortal life children conceived by the Holy Spirit and born of God. . . . " As she
pursues the glory of Christ the Church in fact seeks to become SIMILAR to her whom she invokes as "advocate,
willing helper, mediatrix. . . " (*Lumen Gentium,* 60-64)

*   *   *

One Sunday evening a short while before his death, Father Maximilian gave a lecture on "the relationship between
the Immaculata and the Trinity." Those who survived the
hell of Auschwitz have kept of it an unforgettable memory, of
which they cannot speak without tears. They relate how they
suddenly felt "carried away into the Kingdom of Him who
is Infinite Love." Enraptured, they hung on every word as
Father Maximilian described how the God who is Love
"found a unique response to his Love in the absolutely flawless 'YES' given Him by that masterpiece of creation who
fulfils the expectations of milleniums: the Immaculate Virgin. In her, heaven and earth come together in union, THE
CREATOR'S LOVE AND ALL THE LOVE OF THE
CREATURE whom the Holy Spirit made fruitful forever
and ever in the order of grace. Mother of the Word made
Flesh, of both the Head and Mystical Body, she exists only
in order to give THE LIFE: her Son who by his death conquered death, in whom henceforth we are restored. . . . "

Let us picture this unique scene, Father Maximilian
surrounded by seething, desperate, dying men who are suddenly freed of their fear . . . and their hate, transported by
words that spring from his own intensely lived experience,
into a world where love triumphs forever! A sublime antici-
pation of that passage of LUMEN GENTIUM which exalts
the grandeur of Mary:

"The Virgin Mary, who at the message of the angel received the Word of God in her heart and in her body and
gave to the world THE LIFE . . . the beloved daughter of

185

the Father and temple of the Holy Spirit, she is endowed with the high office and dignity of the Mother of the Son God. Because of this gift of sublime grace she far surpasses all creatures in heaven and on earth. . . . 'She is clearly the mother of the members of Christ . . . since she has by her charity joined in bringing about the birth of believers in the Church, who are members of its head'." (St. Augustine; *Lumen Gentium,* VIII, 53).

*   *   *

In his missionary campaign to push forward the Kingship of Christ the Lord through the Immaculata, Father Maximilian used *materially poor means:* his famous "shells" or supplies of Miraculous Medals with which he filled his pockets, but above all the Rosary which he fingered at length day and night. From this school of contemplation (to which, in the Eastern Church, the "prayer of Jesus" corresponds) his worker sons acquired degrees that would have delighted the Doctor of Nights.†

There again, at the expense of certain theologians whose "unjustified narrowness" he denounced, Vatican II *has proved him right:* "This sacred synod . . . insists that all the Church's sons and daughters generously foster the cult, especially the liturgical cult, of the Blessed Virgin; that they reserve a place of very great importance for the practices and exercises of devotion towards her that the Magisterium of the Church has recommended in the course of centuries, and that they religiously observe those decrees enacted in earlier times regarding the honoring of images of Christ, the Blessed Virgin and the Saints" (*Lumen Gentium,* 67).

This text is ignored by the iconoclasts, but it thrills our brothers in the Eastern Church. Their devotion has preserved flawlessly the great tradition on the public veneration of icons

†St. John of the Cross

codified by the universal Church in the Second Council of Nicea. There again Father Maximilian established ties between the East and the West. Tourists know well the esteem they have over there for the "shells" of Our Lady's "Madman."

* * *

Here he is now upon our altars. We have tried to pass on his message, knowing full well that the essential part of it is unutterable. It is therefore up to our readers to aim their antennas and establish contact! By voluntarily dying in a starvation bunker (which anyone can visit today at Auschwitz-Oswiecim), Father Maximilian wanted to deliver to us the secret of *"the greatest love"*: *the one that gives all, even life itself, for the well-being of one's brothers.*

For those who want their kingdom here on earth, God's love is out of reach. But when a man freely offers his life in sacrifice, this shakes them, moves them, makes them reflect, finishes sometimes by opening their hearts to God who waits at the door as a poor man, and never enters by housebreaking.

Not long before his death, Father Maximilian said to his sons: "there is no heroic act we cannot accomplish with the aid of the Immaculata. . . . What shall be the criterion of our perfection? To do all things as she would do them in our place, and above all to love God as she loves him, with her own heart. . . . THIS IS LEARNED ONLY ON ONE'S KNEES!"

* * *

By his life, but especially by his death, Father Maximilian is an eminently modern saint. In the face of a world without God, or which proclaims the death of God, our theological arguments and our "proofs" for his existence carry little weight: what counts is the TESTIMONY OF A VERY GREAT LOVE.

We are all more or less contaminated by a dialectic that pits those we love against those we do not love. Our "neighbors" are often very select company! Now, according to the unanimous opinion of all who knew him, Father Maximilian did not know hatred. In the full hell of unchained passions he could say: "I HATE NO ONE." He dare urge his sons to love the Germans. "They, too," he said, "are children of the Immaculata."

Never has love been so scoffed at and turned into a caricature as in our times, and never has man had such a hunger and thirst for love: for TRUE love which GIVES itself without receiving a return; which is totally free of self-interest; which opens oneself to the "other" whatever the cost may be.

I had a comrade from my prison days who was sinking in despair. He had lost all faith in man . . . and in God. One day I threw at him as an answer and as a challenge the "case" of Fr. Maximilian Kolbe who died in a starvation bunker for a person he did not even KNOW.

"I defy you to show me a saint in an extermination camp," he had said to me at the end of our argument, "A saint. A real one. One who puts his neighbor ahead of himself. I defy you!"

In writing this book over twenty years ago I took up the challenge.

I do not think it an indiscretion to say that its point-blank thrust hit Pierre, my comrade from prison, full in the heart. Father Maximilian literally bewitched him. As a pilgrim at Oswiecim he renewed the broken bonds. In finding man again, he found God.

*   *   *

In his lifetime Father Maximilian liked to repeat, "On this earth we can work with only one hand, because with the other we must hang on like grim death in order not to fall, ourselves. But in heaven it will be different. No danger of slipping or falling! Then we will work much more, *with both our hands.*"

Father Maximilian, all those who love you and know you are well aware that you keep your word. No one invokes you in vain, and the all-good Virgin grants you immense power. How many graces have been obtained through your intercession, how many cures of the body, and how many resurrections of the soul! Indeed, you have not wasted your time; and now that the Church declares you 'Blessed,' men may trust you as an infallible guide through this rock-strewn world in their arduous ascents toward tomorrow's sun.

Only love conquers hatred; *and in order to preserve faith in God, it is sometimes necessary first to preserve faith in man.* In an age that explores every last circle of despair and fears fellowship like a real hell, you joyously deliver your message of boundless love, your message ratified, not in the serenity of a Franciscan cloister—to which, indeed, you had a right—but in the inhuman horror of a world of concentration camps, a world that cultivates hatred on principle and with a satanic logic.

You belong to our age; you belong to us—wonderfully real and actual. You avoid nothing that presents itself, except sin. You place your confidence in man and his work, in his discoveries and in technical progress, asking only one thing: that he set everything in the proper direction, encompass everything and fuse it all into a hymn of glory to God. Splendidly modern, you place your confidence in Divine Providence, which knows everlastingly how to write straight with the crooked lines of history. You believe with awe in the triumph of the One who has never lost a battle, who reigns from the height of the Cross!

What is your secret? You share it with us: *She through whom all grace comes.* Even more than your words of burning love, your whole life, your death, convinces us, subjugates us. You yourself are the most compelling model of your doctrine. In order to ascend with you, is it not sufficient to place ourselves unreservedly in her spotless hands, to climb rung by rung the steep ascent of that "white ladder"? Only the first step is painful.

At the top of it, the Immaculata is ready to fish for souls —with you as bait.

* * *

And now Pierre, my brother—and all you countless other Pierres who have caught hope from Our Lady's Madman—it is your turn to pass on the flaming torch!

Other Literature on Fr. Maximilian and the Militia of the Immaculata

THE HERO OF AUSCHWITZ A compact 48-page booklet which traces the life of Father Maximilian from his early years to the last days of his life. Good give-away biography for those who do not have time for a full-length book. 35¢

THE LAST DAYS OF MAXIMILIAN KOLBE by S. C. Lorit: Each chapter begins with an account of his last days in Auschwitz Concentration Camp, followed by flashbacks of his whole life. Having access to official documentation and records of eye-witnesses, the author has been able to reconstruct a historically accurate account of the last days of Fr. Maximilian Kolbe. Truly inspirational. Paperback 75¢

Literature in Preparation

THE M.I. IN THE WORDS OF ITS FOUNDER This paperback, excerpted from nine volumes of the critical edition of the writings of Fr. Maximilian, will be an invaluable aid in better understanding the Militia of Mary Immaculate and Mariology in general. For all Marian or Catholic Action groups. Price under a dollar.

RELIGIOUS RENEWAL ACCORDING TO A MODERN DAY SAINT Sparks from the fire of love expressed in Fr. Maximilian's writings and conferences. Topics touched upon: prayer, brotherly love, grace of God and holiness, the Eucharist, fidelity, suffering, apostolate, poverty, obedience, purity and many other admonitions and counsels to raise a soul to perfection. Price under a dollar.

Subscribe to IMMACULATA

IMMACULATA magazine is the M.I. publication for the U.S. Printed and published at "Marytown" by Franciscan Friars who carry on the work of Blessed Maximilian Kolbe in America. The monthly, well-illustrated magazine has a definite Eucharistic and Marian orientation. Not exclusively devotional, it comes to grips with the current problems in the world and in the Church. Its answers to these problems will reflect the mind of the Church as found in Vatican II documents and the Church's visible head, the Pope. Subscription rates, U.S., $5.00 per yr., $9.00—2 yrs., $12.00—3 yrs. Add 50¢ for foreign subscriptions.

Franciscan Marytown Press, 8000 - 39th Ave., Kenosha WI 53141
Phone (414) 694-5118

PROW BOOKLETS

1. **Year of Faith** (Exhortation of Pope Paul VI and U.S. Bishops) — 25¢
2. **Reflections on Conscience & Authority** by Cardinal Wright — 35¢
4. **Penance** (Apostolic Constitution of Pope Paul VI) — 25¢
5. **Our Lady and Vatican II** by William J. Gilligan — 35¢
6. **Lay Spirituality** by John B. Torello — 30¢
7. **Substance of Things Hoped For:** Pope Paul's Reflections on Faith in 1966 — 35¢
8. **The Gift of Faith:** Pope Paul's Reflections on Faith in 1967 — 35¢
10. **A Modern Teenager:** Life of Montserrat Grases — 35¢
11. **Christmas:** 4 Christmas Messages by Pope Paul VI — 35¢
12. **The Penny Catechism:** 270 fundamental questions on the Catholic Faith answered — 35¢
13. **Encounter with Christ in the World** by Msgr. Josemaría Escrivá — 25¢
14. **On Priests and Laity:** an Interview with Msgr. Josemaría Escrivá — 40¢
15. **Woman Today:** an Interview with Msgr. Josemaría Escrivá — 50¢
16. **Human Life:** Encyclical of Pope Paul VI on Marriage — 30¢
17. **The Layman in the Church and in the World** by Fr. Alvaro del Portello. Fr. Portello's commentary on chapter 4 of the "Constitution on the Church" in which the role of the layman is spelled out and his insights into the "Decree on the Apostolate of the Laity" are perhaps the clearest yet published. — 35¢
18. **Credo:** a Profession of Faith by Pope Paul VI — 25¢
19. **Christian Marriage:** Pastoral of the Irish Hierarchy — 35¢
20. **Christian Education:** Education according to Vatican II. Contains encyclical of Pope Pius XI "On the Education of Christian Youth" and "Declaration on Christian Education" — 50¢
21. **Moral Questions for Today:** a statement by the Bishops of England and Wales is masterful. It leaves no doubt in the mind. It states clearly the state of morality in the Western world today. It calls a sin a sin. — 35¢
22. **Abortion: Sexual Suicide** by Jacky Hertz. Mrs. Hertz shows how a woman abandons her very nature when she goes against the law of God, Who in His wisdom designed woman with her nature. — 35¢

Weekly Addresses of Pope Paul VI

For $5 per year you may have the talks of the Holy Father mailed to you each week. The translations are already considered the best English translations and are being used widely. Why depend on short news stories or commentaries on what the Holy Father is saying when for just a few cents and a few minutes each week you can know exactly what the Pope has said. Subscriptions to Canada, Mexico and overseas are $7.50.

Make checks payable to Franciscan Marytown Press and mail to: 8000 - 39th Ave., Kenosha WI 53141. Phone (414) 694-5118